MW01493429

Prais

"Wow, what a book! . . . The stories in this book are heartfelt. Reed has done such a great job in researching and writing this book. . . . I challenge everyone out there to read this book and understand what the rodeo life is all about. . . . I definitely give this book five stars!

—Mindee Brotherson Wilburg,
Customer Service Rep, CentraCom Technology Store, Utah

"All those involved in this sport learn life lessons that carry on for the rest of their lives. I honestly believe that high school rodeo is one of the best extracurricular activities we can have for our young people to be involved with. . . . If we don't keep rodeo in the schools . . . we will soon lose it. Your book can keep the fire burning in those that read it. Thanks for the example you made in the group of people you were involved with."

—Kelly Anderson,
National High School Rodeo Director, Utah

"A shining example of a teacher caring for his students, no matter the circumstances. The book takes me back to simple, genuine caring for adolescents. Teachers truly make a difference."

—Rachelle Matsimuro,
High School Principal, Hawaii

"In the process of entertaining, Reed has brought to the reader's attention the importance of education in and out of the classroom. He has shown that educators can be so influential in the lives of students. Confidence and self-esteem are key ingredients to success, as Thomas so aptly illustrates. Well done!"

—Ruth Nielsen Koenig,
Author, Rodeo Mom, Colorado

"The methods [Reed] used to create interest in rodeo sports follow my main philosophy in sports and education. First, we must help students to be mentally alert; second, to be physical strong; and third, morally acceptable. [The] story of SideKicks is a good and inspiring way to get students involved in helping each other to achieve, to set new goals, and to fit in through team sports."

— Albert Oberlander,
Retired High School Teacher and PE Coach, Wisconsin

"I really enjoyed reading your book. You are so right—boys should be involved in some kind of wholesome activity. My oldest son, Daylon, enjoys the rough-stock events of rodeo, while my younger son, Colton, finds his interest in rodeo's timed events. Your book was inspiring."

—Carrie Swearinger,
New York

SideKicks

Helping Youth Succeed against the Odds

A Teacher's Tale of Grit and Determination

Reed Thomas

Editorial work and production management by Eschler Editing

Cover photo credit: Bryan Strain
(Photo taken at the 2014 Utah High School Rodeo Finals.)
Cover design by Jason Robinson/Bryan Strain
Interior print design and layout by Ben Welch
eBook design and layout by Eugene Woodbury

Published by Scrivener Books (info@scrivenerbooks.com)

First Edition: April 2016
Printed in the United States of America

10 9 8 7 6 5 4 3 2

ISBN 978-0-9895523-9-4

To the SideKicks: without them,
this story would not have happened.
To my wife: without her encouragement and support,
this story would not have been written.

Contents

Foreword

Educators who make a difference in the lives of students are not in the business for the salary. Their joy is in seeing their efforts influence students in positive ways.

And what you will find in the story of the SideKicks is a wonderful example of a master teacher at work. Reed Thomas truly cared about a struggling segment of our school society, the charge of which he accepted as his responsibility.

I well remember the discussion I had with Reed Thomas and other teachers working with such students. Our concerns were centered on ways to motivate these kids—how to get them involved, interested in school, and confident in their own abilities. What came from that discussion was the concept of achievement. One of the great secrets of a happy life is the notion that all of us need to be successful in life more frequently than we fall short.

We knew there would be individual failures and disappointments, but we wanted to inspire our students. Reed Thomas captured the vision of what his students needed. When life got them down, he knew they needed to get back up and continue to try for success. His encouragement and genuine concern for the individual instilled a no-quit attitude in his students, which has helped them in all aspects of their lives.

All in all, Reed's students—especially those who chose to become SideKicks—discovered what all of us must do to know joy and happiness in this life: we must face challenges, overcome fears and negative attitudes, and risk failure and disappointment in order to achieve. Reed did what great mentors always do—he made heroes out of his students.

—Jim Thornton, Educator and Administrator

Preface

My decision to finally write the story of the SideKicks was cemented by two pivotal points in my life.

The first came when I visited the grave of one SideKick on a beautiful spring morning in May 2013. My mind raced back to the year Clint Lynch was a freshman in high school and I was his rodeo advisor. As I stood by his grave, memories of so many adventures with Clint came to life.

Clint's tombstone features an etching of him riding #155, a bull at the State High School Rodeo Finals. The back side of his tombstone is engraved with a pair of spurs, a couple of horseshoes, and the names of his wife and children. His blue eyes, readymade smile, and easygoing, likeable personality are still vivid in my memory. I can still see his black cowboy hat with its bucking bull emblem pinned to the front of the crown. Clint died at the young age of thirty-four, in an accident with his truck while gathering wood—the same age I was when I became his rodeo advisor.

Rodeo had seemed to elevate him to a higher level of self-acceptance, self-worth, and renewed hope for a bright future. And Clint made the most of that opportunity, becoming a two-time qualifier to the State High School Rodeo Finals in bull riding.

Years later, as sorrowing loved ones and his community gathered around Clint's casket, my attention was drawn to several SideKicks coming toward us. Kevin, Rusty, and Kelly soon joined us at the grave site, cowboy hats in hand. That day, each of us SideKicks experienced a special connection, and I found myself surrounded by friends who seemed more like family.

Clint's brothers were also SideKicks. "Speaking at Clint's funeral was one of the most difficult things I have ever done," his brother Val told me. "He was one of the best friends I have ever had. Even though it was tough, it was also a great honor." As I listened to him and talked with my other SideKicks, I was struck with the realization that these stories and experiences needed to be shared with a new generation. Not just for the sake of history or posterity—which would be reason enough—but also for the impact they could make on others.

Now, more than thirty-five years later, the SideKicks have shared their thoughts about the positive effects that intervention had on their lives.

My experiences as an educator cover a thirty-seven-year span of my life, in which I had the privilege of connecting with students in three states as a teacher in the public school system. My students came from various nationalities, interests, talents, and abilities. Six of my most unforgettable years are captured on the pages of SideKicks.

In those years I was given the opportunity to reach out to some high school kids who were unengaged in school. My assignment was to help them become motivated—to enable them to leave high school with a diploma in hand.

And so we introduced a program the kids could be involved in and could call their own, where they felt like they were making a difference. And a miracle happened. Attendance improved, self-worth skyrocketed, and a can-do mentality replaced negative thinking.

The second pivotal moment came one day as I walked beneath an arch made of 8,484 shoes in the nearby community of Fairview. Soberingly, these shoes represented the number of youth in custody in the state of Utah during 2013. That arch sent chills down my spine—chills that intensified as I later learned about the increasing number of suicides among our young people today. I was struck by the cry for help that these shoes represent. And it got me thinking of how the positive experiences of the SideKicks might find a new generation of young people to lift up.

Knowing we made a difference before, it is my hope that in sharing our story we can make a difference again. To paraphrase Mahatma Gandhi, we must all strive to be the change we wish to see in the world."[1]

—Reed Thomas

Introduction

When I think of the qualities of men and women from the "Greatest Generation," I think of the men and women who voluntarily risked their lives to rid the world of evil as soon as they became adults. Some were even willing to buckle themselves into a seat atop a Saturn V launch rocket pointed toward the stars and literally shoot for the moon. In that generation, an entire nation aspired to take risks and achieve greatness.

Greatness requires hard work, selflessness, risk, and sacrifice. As with similar extracurricular activities, Rodeo is a breeding ground for all those qualities.

I recently attended the PRCA Champions Challenge in Spanish Fork, Utah. It was the first professional event I'd ever been to that started with prayer before honoring our flag. The athletes tipped their hats to the crowd rather than thumping their chests at their rivals. The competitors were friendly rather than bitter toward each other.

I was even more impressed when I attended the 2014 Utah State High School Rodeo Finals in Heber City, Utah. A special-needs boy stepped into the arena to sing the national anthem. The crowd was silent with a respect that is sometimes lacking for the more typical performances in events of this size. This boy sang with his chin held high; his body may have lacked in musical ability, but his spirit was able to touch the hearts of the crowd. As he finished the final notes, the crowd cheered as though they had witnessed a musical genius because it was not about them—it was about that boy and his needs. It was about recognizing the willingness of the least capable contributing to the spirit of greatness that still lives in each of our souls.

This spirit continued throughout the event. Other special-needs students participated in races and events in different ways. This type of encouragement didn't only apply to the special-needs students. Every student who participated received recognition from the announcer and crowd. Some students were announced as having excellent grades. And after hearing a few of the honor-roll announcements, I was pleasantly surprised to hear the announcer state, "This young man's greatest accomplishment is that he got passing grades in all of his classes." There wasn't an ounce of sarcasm in his voice. Having been an unmotivated student myself in high school, I understand that this was an accomplishment every bit as worthy as the others. Each time a similar announcement came over the sound system, I rejoiced that this youth had been spared failure by participating in high school rodeo.

That's why the stories in this book are so important. Our youth often need more than they are currently getting from our culture, schools, and sometimes even families. They need something to build their confidence, motivate them, and teach them how to work hard so they can become proud of who they are. They need to be taught how to be great.

My hope is that the stories in this book will inspire and motivate parents, teachers, school administrators, and the community at large to come together and develop programs and resources to similarly help our kids succeed against the odds. We need to support things that will teach youth how to work hard, sacrifice, believe in themselves and others—in short, to become great. Why? Because youth who develop these character traits will be part of a new greatest generation.

—Bryan Strain

CHAPTER ONE

A Decision

A Lesson Learned: Listen to Your Sixth Sense

Was I supposed to move or stay where I was? I felt squeezed between a rock and a hard place. This decision would have a lasting effect on my family—and maybe even on many others in ways I couldn't yet see. It was daunting. I finally decided to rely on my "sixth sense"—my inner prompting, my gut. I would take it one step at a time and trust that things would work out as they should.

I had recently finished a master's degree program at Northern Arizona University and had become involved with the University of Nevada Las Vegas and their student-teacher placement program in the school where I was teaching. One of the student teachers had grown up in the Bronx and another in inner-city Houston. Connecting with them and my coworkers, who also came from all walks of life, provided an interesting contrast to my rural upbringing. It was fascinating to work with people from such diverse backgrounds.

My career as an educator had become my way of life, but at heart, I was still a cowboy. While I enjoyed working for the school district in Las Vegas, I increasingly missed the rural lifestyle in which I had been reared. The previous summer in Utah, I had helped my father harvest both the hay on his small cattle ranch and on my own for the small beef cattle operation

I had purchased near my hometown. Being able to teach in Las Vegas and also spend time on my ranch gave me the best of both worlds, but my wife and I had started talking about moving back to my roots. She found my hometown of Wales, Utah—with its population of approximately 250—an interesting contrast to Los Angeles, where she had been reared.

Teaching in Las Vegas was an adventure. Several of my students' parents worked in the entertainment industry, and they sometimes arranged for celebrities to come to our classroom. On one occasion, Mr. Universe came to demonstrate his strength. We watched as he lifted a petite girl off a table using his teeth to grip a belt wrapped around her waist. We also enjoyed a visit with Muhammad Ali and George Foreman prior to their fight to determine the world heavyweight boxing champion. During a field trip to Caesar's Palace, we saw a rock that had been brought back from the moon. Because our school was located in the entertainment capital of the world, we enjoyed many of these unique kinds of experiences.

As I was teaching class one morning in November 1975, the principal opened the door to my room and told me there was a long-distance phone call for me in his office. He offered to stay with my class while I took the call. As I walked toward the office, I was worried it might bad news from a parent or other relative. With that in mind, the walk to the office seemed especially long, and I quickened my step.

By the time I picked up the receiver and said hello, my heart was pounding against my chest.

"Is this Reed Thomas?" the caller asked. When I confirmed my identity, he said, "This is Mr. Blackham from the North Sanpete School District. There's a teaching position opening at our high school, and we need to establish a program that will encourage students to remain in school and to graduate. We can't find anyone in the district willing to fill the position. We were wondering if you might be interested."

I was stunned into silence. My initial reaction was profound relief that no one in my family had passed away. Almost immediately, certain thoughts flashed through my mind. They wanted me to teach at North Sanpete High, the school from which I had graduated in 1959. And they wanted me to help kids stay in school. Back in the day, if a boy wasn't a member of the Hawks Club at North Sanpete, he didn't quite fit in— and, as was typical of most rural American high schools, many clubs were by invitation only. I had belonged to FFA and had enjoyed it, but that hadn't given me the acceptance I craved. I imagined that some of the boys currently at North Sanpete found themselves in a similar situation.

Though I was enjoying my associations with my colleagues and students in Las Vegas, I couldn't deny missing my "country boy" lifestyle. But what about my job? I was under contract with the Clark County School District for the entire school year—and didn't even know if I could leave.

Amid all those conflicting thoughts, I realized Mr. Blackham was on the other end of the line waiting for some kind of response.

"May I let you know tomorrow?" I stammered. "I really need to talk this over with my principal and my wife."

Mr. Blackham agreed and assured me he would be waiting for my call.

I immediately felt conflict raging in my gut. Would a move to Utah be good for us as a family, or would it be better to stay and rear our family in Nevada? The first thing that came to my mind was money. At that time, teacher pay was much better in the Clark County School District than in rural Utah. Moving would represent a pay cut of a few thousand dollars. But I also knew that houses were cheaper in Utah.

Almost immediately I found myself wrestling with another thought. How was I going to tell my principal? We had a good working relationship, and I hated to ask him to release me from my responsibilities—especially since we were already a couple of months into a new school year.

My fears were well-founded. When I broke the news to Mr. Roundy, he was not pleased.

"I am not going to release you," he said. "I prefer to have you keep your contract with us."

That must be my answer, I thought. I guess it's meant for us to stay in Las Vegas.

I decided that was probably okay and began to think of all the advantages staying in Las Vegas entailed. The lifestyle was exciting. We had made some close friends while living there. It was only a six-hour drive to my hometown in Utah, and so I could enjoy both worlds. Best of all, I wouldn't need to take a pay cut. With each succeeding thought, the conflict in my gut started to ease.

That settled feeling was short-lived, however. The next day, Mr. Roundy approached me and said, "Reed, we have decided to release you from your contract, if that's what you want." I thanked him, and my thoughts of the previous day were shoved into the backseat. I immediately felt peaceful about accepting the teaching offer in Utah. I decided to put my faith in a higher power, which I believe helped me to move toward another purpose in my life's journey.

After making phone calls first to my wife and then to Mr. Blackham, and then saying good-bye to my students and close friends, I began preparing for a new adventure in rural Utah.

CHAPTER TWO

A New Assignment (1975)

A Lesson Learned: Don't Be Judgmental

Normal?

Who is, what is . . . normal?
Webster describes normal as
"ordinary, average, usual,
having average intelligence,
normalcy."
We all have a common bond of DNA
From the beginning to the present.
What pushes a person on the
 Battlefield to risk one's life
To rescue a fallen soldier?
To jump out of a perfectly
Good plane to guide to
Earth with nothing but a parachute?
To plunge into the corporate
World or into politics,
A doctor—a lawyer—the
Blue-collar workforce,
Engines that drive us all.
The homeless in their cardboard castles—
Mental wards filled with normalcy

To less than . . .
From staff to resident, I believe
We are all normal.
Normal to doubt, normal to question,
Normal to succeed.
Remember, when we judge those around us,
We are all just "normal."

—Jerald King

MOUNT PLEASANT, a city with a population of just over three thousand, was a place where everybody could feel like somebody. On Friday nights, the community came together to watch the Hawks play ball. Even when I was a student there, high school sports was what kept the community alive.

The town served as the hub of several outlying smaller communities in an area I felt was a great place to rear a family. As soon as we arrived, I realized how deep my roots went. I was back where I had been born, reared, and educated.

The day I started my new job, however, I wondered if I should have stayed in Las Vegas. North Sanpete High School had a student enrollment of fewer than five hundred. It was a typical American rural high school, steeped in tradition, and I immediately realized that it was going to be difficult—maybe impossible?—to break some of the traditions causing students to flounder. Then I reminded myself that my sixth sense had brought me back, making this assignment a mission of sorts.

Soon after my arrival, I found that the principal and several members of his teaching staff were more than a bit leery of my "mission." It was obvious they did not want change. My allies were the district office administrators who had hired me and the vice principal, who had been assigned to be my support. Being caught in the battle between the old and the new, I often arrived home feeling stressed. It felt good to have my small farm as a getaway.

Even with the conflict, I respected my principal and the teachers who opposed me. The principal was a good man, the teachers good teachers. I just felt a little sorry that the welcome mat had not been laid out.

It occurred to me that they may have resented the government interaction. In those days, there was very little government control over education. Until federal money started being used to fund education, parents and local school board members had most of the control. I remembered reading what Bill Gates had said: "Education reform is tougher than battling polio, malaria, and tuberculosis." He'd also said that "the one thing we have a lot of in the United States is unmotivated students." And I had been hired to motivate students.[2]

Mr. Blackham told me that one of my responsibilities would be to test students referred to me by teachers. These would be students whose academic performance indicated they weren't on track for graduation. I knew that some of these students were unhappy with school and had just about given up, and that started to weigh on me. I wanted to make a difference in their lives, to help them change apathy to motivation. It soon became apparent that some were underestimating their true potential, their talents, and even their intellectual ability.

I will never forget an experience I had as I finished testing a freshman referred to me by his math teacher. He had a high IQ yet was struggling in math. After the testing, we got together and discussed the results.

"You have a good head on your shoulders," I told him.

"I do?" he responded with disbelief.

I pointed out the average norm on the graph, then showed him he was far above it. He seemed surprised and became silent, appearing deep in thought. Then he shared his story with me: "When I was in the third grade, a teacher put me in a lower level in her class. I decided I was not very smart and that something was wrong with me. I just gave up trying to learn. I began watching time pass on the clock." Once I showed him his test results, he got a glimpse of his true potential. His senior year, he represented North Sanpete High School at the regional math competition at Brigham Young University.

Some of the students had been hurt by words—words that cut so deep it caused them to withdraw. They were the ones who seemed to be shy, who were loners, the ones who had few, if any, friends. I had been a student in this school district, and I knew that kids in this small, rural community could be cliquish. Many felt driven to protect a certain image. If a student wasn't part of a group, he stood alone, for few, if any, were about to reach out and invite that student to join their group or club. One such student ended up taking his own life after he left school. To this day I feel the pain his parents endured simply because no one reached out to him.

Some students were extremely soft-spoken, which was somewhat typical for this rural area. They offered a lot of "yep" and "nope" answers but little else. At first, few were willing to hold a conversation with me as an adult—also a fairly typical thing. Once I had established a rapport with them, though, they started opening up.

Most of the students I tested had average or higher IQs. However, they sometimes showed a deficit in math or one of the English language art areas. Once we got their test results, our teachers started realizing how intelligent these kids were— even gifted in some areas. However, the question remained— Why were they not experiencing success in class?

I often reflected on my own father's experience. Each night, he'd sit in his chair, struggling to read the newspaper, yet I knew he was a smart man. Despite his limited education and finances, he'd put together a cattle business that provided well for a family of six. When he died, he left behind considerable wealth. It was his self-esteem and self-confidence that had given him the desire to press forward despite his limited ability to read.

Measuring intelligence seemed to be rather complex. I began to wonder how many different kinds of intelligence and abilities were left unmeasured and unrecognized. I even wondered what effect poverty and socioeconomic status had on an IQ test score. Four decades later, I have come to the conclusion that test scores are only part of a very big and complicated picture. From my current vantage point, I can see that some of the students who seemed most likely to succeed still have not reached their expected mark. On the other hand, some who were not expected to succeed have excelled far above expectation.

Some teachers had even given up on the students they had referred to me. I sometimes heard disparaging comments as I ate lunch in the faculty lounge: "We don't want those kids in the Hawks Club; they would go against our training rules." "We ought to just boot them out." "The outside world does not put up with this nonsense, why should we?" "Those damn kids were just like this in junior high. I didn't expect them to change." "Students that can't measure up should be dropped from school and forced into the outside world."

To remove myself from the negativity, I began eating lunch in my classroom by myself. I chose to follow Mark Twain's advice: "Keep away from people who try to belittle ambitions. Small people always do that, but the really great make you feel that you, too, can become great."[3]

It suddenly occurred to me that some of these students could be the first in their families to attend college. That struck me with particular force, as I was a first-generation college student myself. I would have lost that opportunity had it not been for a family who'd pointed me in a more positive direction. With that realization, I began envisioning something better for students who seemed to have the smarts but lacked the motivation to excel.

When I looked at these students, I saw good boys with great potential, which, on the surface, was sometimes difficult to see. Several of these students just had an adventurous side, while others appeared to be full of "piss and vinegar." One student, Bert Miner, decided to make a cannon in shop class. He fashioned it on the lathe out of aluminum and filled it full of powder with a .22 slug. After school, he and his buddies took it to a neighboring community's livestock slaughterhouse, where they fired it. Bert said, "I drilled the hole a little off center. When I lit the fuse, the cannon spun around. The slug got me in the right upper arm. I still have the scar. Other than that, my arm doesn't bother me." When I heard about it, I thought, *Boys will be boys.*

A group of my students—the more adventurous ones— once rode their horses more than forty miles over the top of a mountain range to watch a rodeo. They called it a "pack trip." When they arrived, they were allowed to enter the rodeo free since they were on horseback—a good thing since they probably had little or no money. After the rodeo they slept on the dirt racetrack that surrounded the rodeo grounds. It was another forty-mile horseback ride home; only by the time they left, it was raining. They arrived home safely but soaked.

On another occasion, these same students gathered a herd of bulls from a local pasture in the middle of the night and drove them to the rodeo arena. There, they took turns climbing aboard the bulls in the bucking chute and riding them out into the arena under the light of the moon. Afterward they returned the bulls to the pasture without the owner ever knowing anything had happened.

I wondered what I could do to help these enterprising but educationally unmotivated youth to reach beyond their cir-cumstances and self-imposed prisons. It was obvious the most important thing happening at the school was athletics. Foot-ball ruled. I certainly recognized the importance of high school sports, athletic clubs, drill teams, cheerleaders, and all other athletic-related activities. They had their benefits, including bringing the community together and providing a natural high for youth, students, faculty, and parents. My biggest concern, however, was for students not involved in athletics or any other extracurricular activities. I believed that if they were involved in something, it would help them establish an identity, build self-esteem, and give them a sense of belonging. Beyond that, they would experience some fun.

It needed to happen now. I will never forget the student who one day had been making everyone in my classroom laugh and the next was found dead, having hung himself. I had known life was tough for him. Was there something more I could have done to help him? I didn't know for sure, but if I could make a difference for other kids who were struggling, I was determined to find a way.

As I contemplated what to do, memories of my own youth began to flood my mind. My father had taught me how to drive his Studebaker pickup at an early age. Early on, I would sit on his lap as I drove. Later, I discovered I could reach the clutch if I really stretched my left leg. Then I discovered I could change gears with that stick shift on the floor. I could even see over the steering wheel by stretching my neck a bit.

I was my father's sidekick. We went most everywhere together. After a local rodeo, it was to the closest beer joint. My father enjoyed the taste of alcohol. While he was inside, I would sleep in the truck, his horse in the back keeping me company. Every once in a while my father or one of his drinking buddies would bring me out some candy. At closing time, my father would be "three sheets to the wind," and I would be the designated driver.

During my teenage years, I began experimenting with alcohol. It started with a gallon of cheap wine shared by three of us at the Sophomore Swing. Someone at the dance cut off my tie with a pair of scissors. I remember enjoying the attention I was getting from some of my classmates while I was under the influence.

To celebrate my high school graduation, those same two friends and I had each purchased a fifth of Jim Beam whiskey. At three o'clock in the morning, I passed out. I should have died of alcohol poisoning. I seemed to be on a road to self-destruction, but a higher power must have known I had a reason to live— perhaps a mission to fulfill.

Not long after that near-death experience, my life started taking a different path. After high school graduation, I began dating a girl two years younger than I was. She was a religious girl, as were her parents. Her life had focus; mine did not. I am still amazed that her parents even allowed her to go out with me. She and her parents helped me get my life headed in a direction where I began to forget self and serve others.

From personal experience, I knew alcohol consumption could wreak havoc in a student's life, affecting almost every aspect of it, especially academics. I wanted to find a way to help students avoid addiction, but I also knew that sometimes the only way to find the right path was to learn the harsh lessons of going down the wrong path. I wanted to give back what had been given to me. I had been given a gift, and as I remembered the positive influence of that teenage girl and her family, I wanted to do the same for others. And now I found myself in an optimal position to do just that.

The great educator Booker T. Washington once said, "Wherever our life touches yours, we help or hinder . . . wherever your life touches ours, you make us stronger or weaker. There is no escape—man drags man down or man lifts man up."[4] I desperately wanted to lift others.

I felt that some students were only difficult because no one had developed an intervention and/or the necessary teaching skills to lift them above the status quo. I wanted them to enjoy school. I remembered a book I had read in elementary school—*Smoky the Cowhorse,* by Will James—that left a lasting impression on me. Smoky had become a difficult horse to handle, but through Clint's intervention, Smoky became a good cow horse. In fact, he became "the best cow horse in the whole outfit."[5] On the road to success, Smoky had gone through some mighty tough times, much like some of the students at North Sanpete.

Remembering the book and its message, I started seeing that some of the students considered difficult by teachers actually had great potential. With the right opportunities, they could be successful. We just needed to find a vehicle to help students find success not only in school but in life itself. With Will James's story as a model, I began searching for something that could provide incentive, not only to finish high school with a diploma, but also to have some fun along the way.

CHAPTER THREE

A Vehicle

A Lesson Learned: Persistence Pays

SOME OF THE STUDENTS at North Sanpete High School wanted to start a high school rodeo club. Back then, there were no such programs in our area. High school rodeo clubs existed in Utah, but none were connected directly to any high school curriculum. Our students, though, wanted a high school rodeo club that was part of their school, and so they started circulating a petition.

Even today high school rodeo is called that because it is open to high-school-age students. It would be unique to have a rodeo program at a high school that had been adopted and supported by a school board.

Again, I thought back to my own high school experience. During my freshman year, I became interested in basketball and even made the team. But I had a problem: I was getting home late when I had farm chores to do. My father gave me no support with athletics; he said we had more important things to do than play ball, things like feeding livestock and breaking colts.

My father enjoyed the life of a cowboy; he was a ranch type who'd ridden broncs and roped calves in his younger days. I identified with his lifestyle. He supported me more in my cowboy interests than he did in my ball playing. Under his tutelage, I learned how to ride horses and colts and to rope.

Because of my cowboy experiences, I connected with the students who wanted the support of the local school board for a high school rodeo club. But no one would have guessed I felt that way—after all, I had just moved to Mount Pleasant from Las Vegas and had married a girl from Los Angeles. And my attire would never have hinted that I was a cowboy. Compared to the shorter hairstyles of the male teachers at North Sanpete, my hair was rather long, which had been the style among male teachers in Las Vegas.

I was much like the student who was half Navajo, half Caucasian. After visiting his grandmother on the reservation in Arizona, he told me that she had called him *Lichii Bilasaana*, or "red apple"—red on the outside and white on the inside. It occurred to me that I appeared to be city on the outside while I was very much country on the inside.

Mr. Thornton, our vice principal, approached me one day and told me about the petition for the high school rodeo program. He asked that I serve as their advisor. His request was remarkable in more ways than one. Ours was a typical rural high school, where sports, namely football, ruled—a fact clearly demonstrated by our trophy case.

Despite that, I enthusiastically agreed to the request. Here was the vehicle I had been searching for! Almost immediately some frightening images entered my mind. What if a student got seriously injured on a bull or bronc? I had seen some *bad* injuries in rodeo. The string of what-ifs battered my resolve. On the other hand, I knew people got injured playing football. I concluded I wouldn't live in fear and that this was not the time to dwell on negatives. I needed to think positively and follow my gut. And, lo and behold, we succeeded. Rodeo became an official extracurricular activity at North Sanpete High School.

I began to see that rodeo provided the opportunity for more students at North Sanpete to experience natural highs. Rodeo could build one's self-confidence. It could even create positive labels and motivate students to earn their high school diplomas. Looking at the positives, I began to feel we had experienced nothing short of a miracle.

It was time to get started. However, I knew very little about high school rodeo at the time. I had heard that it had its beginning in Texas. And one of my students told me that his father, Jim Young, had won the National High School Finals Rodeo Bareback Bronc Riding Championship in 1965. And that was it—my entire base of information about high school rodeo.

My first item of business was to make it clear that high school rodeo, as an extracurricular activity at North Sanpete, was open to *any* high school student who wanted to participate. Any high-school-age student who wanted to be a member of the North Sanpete High School Rodeo Club could join.

We did everything we needed for rodeo to become an official program at the high school. We wrote bylaws we adopted from the national high school rules. And the students came up with our name—SideKicks. It didn't refer to the kind of sidekick Tonto was to the Lone Ranger or the kind I was to my father. They called themselves SideKicks because they rode bucking horses, bulls, and performance horses and delivered kicks to the sides of their animals.

Elections were held March 1976. Glen Terry, also known as "Shorty," became the first club president, with Rusty Bench as vice president, Karen Anderson as secretary, and Casey Black-burn as treasurer. These officers were some of the first contestants to represent North Sanpete High School. To be a rodeo contestant, you had to have passing grades in all classes and had to conduct yourself according to the requirements of the State Athletic Association. And that wasn't all. To enter an approved high school rodeo, you had to be enrolled in the insurance program approved by the National High School Rodeo directors. You also had to pay membership dues. Additionally, you had to get a parent's signature and have it notarized for every rodeo you entered. The principal's signature was also required to attest that you had passing grades in all classes. We also adopted all other rules set by the state and national high school rodeo associations.

The local newspaper carried our story with the headline "New Rodeo Club at North Sanpete High" (see appendix). We were off and running!

CHAPTER FOUR

Connecting

A Lesson Learned: Fun Stimulates Learning

Silver and Sliver

A country bumpkin set forth to make his mark in life,
Assigned treasure of tarnished currency.
Kicked through the halls of education,
Ending up hopeless in front of him.
Reaching back to his roots,
Relying on cowboy intellect taught by his father.
Soiled clothes, much easier to clean
Than souls dirtied from living.
Put together the high school's first rodeo club,
"SideKicks" was its name.
With a couple of mascots, Silver and Sliver,
They learned parts of the rope from dummies.
Greatness appeared little by little,
Coil by coil, loop by loop.

—Jerald King

CREATING A RELATIONSHIP with those rural high school students was initially challenging. My students saw me as nothing more than a city dude—until I brought my lariat to class. I set up a chair and roped it a few times. They were amazed I knew how to rope. Soon I started teaching interested students how to rope.

I found myself teaching in the same classroom where I had studied high school biology sixteen years earlier—a room located front and center, right at the heart of the school. What a contrast! I never could have predicted it. I was teaching students how to rope before and after class.

Demonstrating the swing and delivery, I began teaching students the different parts of a lariat: the hondo, the spoke, the lope. I taught them how to feed the loop. I showed them the proper way to coil the lariat and how to release only enough coils to make the catch. I taught them how to handle the remaining coils in their hand.

I coached the students until they were able to catch our dummy calf on a regular basis. We even practiced the "dally"—wrapping the rope around the saddle horn. I also taught the heel throw. Before long we were team roping a dummy in that classroom, its high ceiling coming in mighty handy for those roping activities.

Soon attitudes changed and interest skyrocketed. Students started calling me Reed rather than Mr. Thomas. Some teachers felt that calling a teacher by their first name was disrespectful, but against their protests, I allowed it to continue—I felt it encouraged a connection between me and the students. I even had some new students call me Mr. Reed, thinking my first name was my last name.

I saw enthusiasm soar. Before and after classes, the students moved desks aside to make room for a small roping area. One student welded an iron horse in shop class. He painted it silver, we placed a saddle on it, and gave it a name: Silver. We also built a dummy calf from an old rayon tire to which we attached wooden legs; the students named him Sliver, probably because his wooden legs produced a sliver or two.

I showed the students how to do two wraps and a "hooey" with a "pigging" string. The hooey is a couple of wraps and a half hitch and is used to tie a calf's legs together in tie-down roping; the pigging string is the small rope used for the tie. The cowboy makes two compete wraps around three of the calf's legs; next, he makes an additional wrap around two of those legs, finishing off by bringing the rope up under the last wrap. A timer proved that there were some mighty fast catches and ties in that classroom; I saw times that were right up with the rodeo-arena pros.

Students who had been getting to school late were now arriving early. I loved the feedback I was getting:

"Coming into this classroom is great. It's fun to jump on Silver and rope Sliver."

"This rests my brain from other classes; it's fun."

"This contraption makes us want to come to school. It's fun and exciting."

"It builds our self-confidence when we rope it."

"This horse and calf give me something to do after school when I am waiting for the bus. It helps us to learn to rope."

"I like this class because it teaches me how to rope, and I can use these skills on the farm. Someday, I may be a calf roper or a team roper! This is my favorite class."

"People may not think this is fun, but when you see yourself improving, it becomes fun. You begin to feel good about yourself. It gives us something to do before class begins."

"It gives kids a chance to unwind."

"It brings a little laughter."

"It helps kids realize that after several tries, success does come."

"It gives kids something to look forward to at school."

"It is a lot easier to get up in the morning when you have something fun to do."

"I have even heard a *yee-haw!* When is the last you felt that happy?"

As I read their comments, I realized I had begun to hear laughter as I watched and participated in these roping contests. I felt tremendous energy within the walls of that classroom.

Despite the obvious positive impact on students, the principal didn't seem to appreciate what I was doing. I remember one occasion when he and another person peeked into my classroom. I walked over to the door as they began walking down the hall, and I overheard the principal say, "That teacher may spell trouble—he just moved up here from Las Vegas."

But I was undeterred, spurred on by the enthusiasm my students were showing. We didn't stop with Silver and Sliver. To give students an opportunity to experience the feel of a bucking bull, we built a bucking barrel at the edge of the high school football field. With this homemade device, the SideKicks were able to get an idea of what it felt like to ride a bull. That barrel could not only buck, it also rolled somewhat like a bull. Robert Draper was one of the first to climb aboard.

Our fifty-gallon barrel, with its ropes tied to heavy-duty springs, did look rather out of place at the edge of the football field. But the most important thing was the building of self-confidence among boys who had not been invited to join the

Hawks Club. It gave them something to look forward to. None of us were bothered about what other students—and even some teachers—thought. Most amazing to me was the fact that it was not my six-plus years of college and university classes that were valuable in my new endeavor but the teachings of my father.

As the weeks and months went by, our club had a tremendous impact. Even potential dropouts now wanted to stay in school. The kids felt like they had a new lease on life. They were smiling and laughing. They were buckling down and studying harder so they could get better grades. It wasn't just that they were having fun—it was that, for possibly the first time, they had a vision, a reason to want to get their assignments done.

A few of the teachers bristled as I began breaking high school tradition. However, I had seen some great teachers use their gifts and talents to reach students in their own unique ways. One teacher gifted in music used that talent to foster interest and to make things fun. Another used cartoon drawings. Since I could neither sing, play a musical instrument, nor draw, I used a lariat.

After the Christmas holidays of 1975, I noticed that several students were wearing cowboy hats to school. They were all Stetsons—high-quality felt hats. It was rather obvious what they'd gotten for Christmas. Soon I started hearing that some teachers were annoyed with the hats in the classroom. But almost as soon as I heard about the complaints, one of my students presented a solution: John built a hat rack in his shop class out of a metal pipe, a metal stand, and horseshoes. It was painted orange and placed by the door of my classroom for easy access. Since it was 1976, someone placed a bicentennial sticker on it. And just like that, my classroom became the cowboy-hat hang-up.

The SideKicks started getting pumped up about high school rodeo. The boys participating that first year came from different backgrounds and circumstances, but their cowboy hats and boots told the world they were a team. No one had to guess what club they represented. They began finding that they had renewed hopes, dreams, and desires as they developed a unique bond with their teammates. And they weren't the only ones: I found myself reliving some of my teenage years through them and dreaming big on their behalf.

Best of all, they kept the door open for anyone who wanted to join their club.

CHAPTER FIVE

Meet Some SideKicks

A Lesson Learned: Value Unique Gifts and Talents

WHEN IT COMES to athletes, there's no doubt rodeo cowboys are some of the toughest around. The sport requires physical and mental toughness, and the willingness to face fear and take risks.[6] The average football player wouldn't last long in any of the rodeo events. Knowing this, I began to wonder which of my students had what it took to be a North Sanpete High School rodeo competitor. I figured only time would tell.

We'd had lots of fun roping in the classroom and riding our barrel at the edge of the football field, but it took a special kind of grit to get bucked off a bull or bronc, get trampled, dust yourself off, and get back on. I knew it would be a new challenge for the SideKicks.

Danny Livingston was the first SideKick to represent North Sanpete High School at a rodeo. Danny had grown up with a father who was a bricklayer. He had developed a strong arm, which probably helped him hang on while sitting atop a bucking horse. He had a pleasant, likeable personality and was always willing to lend a helping hand, but he also seemed to enjoy a little adventure and had a mischievous side as well. With a taste for living on the edge, riding broncs was right up his alley.

Casey Blackburn, a member of the high school's radio class, worked at the class station, Radio KMTP–FM, and had a little rhythm in his bones. He was also a member of the school choir. Casey's father, Dee, could play the guitar and carry a pretty decent tune, so he must have passed on some of his musical talent to Casey, who used his sense of rhythm atop a bucking animal. Dee and my father had both been members of a roping club. After calf-roping practices, they would occasionally get together for a little entertainment with Dee doing the picking and singing. I don't know whether Casey's mother could sing, but she did try her best to talk him out of riding bronc horses. She wanted him to stay with radio rather than rodeo. Casey said, "She was afraid that I might get hurt. When I told her there were more injuries in football than rodeo, she finally gave in."

Rusty Bench could sing a song, and he had a natural ability in picking up the rhythm of a bucking bull or bronc. He was also a theatrical talent, playing the role of Sir Edward Ramsey in *The King and I* and the leading role of Professor Higgins in *My Fair Lady*. I can still see him as Professor Higgins, wearing that black moustache under his cowboy hat. Rusty played football as a guard for the Hawks, but it was high school rodeo—especially bull riding—that really seemed to hold his attention.

Soft-spoken Glen Terry went by the name of "Shorty" all through school, and he still does. The nickname had stuck in kindergarten, where he'd been the shortest kid. Everyone seemed to like him. When I asked him how he'd felt about school before he became a SideKick, he said, "I never really wanted to go to school. When I became a member of the SideKicks, I had something to look forward to every day, and I learned how to be positive no matter what. Being a member of the rodeo club changed my attitude toward school."

In high school Glen was only five-feet-four, weighed a slight 125 pounds, and wore a size 6 7/8 hat. Glen's father, Ross, said, "In Little League, the pitcher was six feet tall; Shorty, as catcher, was eight inches shorter. But he was a good catcher. When you put those two next to each other, they made an interesting contrast."

Ross maintained that Shorty was the biggest little man he ever knew—and, as he often said, "It's not the size of the man in the fight but the size of the fight in the man." As an example of his toughness, he was among the boys who'd ridden their horses forty miles to that rodeo in Huntington and then back home in the rain.

When I pointed out that Shorty seemed like a natural at riding rough stock, his father replied, "At the kids' rodeo out in Birdseye, he would often land on his feet and win. Even when he was very young, you could drop him and he would land on his feet, just like a cat. You couldn't knock him off his feet, and he never knew what fear was." One local rodeo cowboy said that Shorty had the most natural ability of any bull rider he had ever seen.

And then there was Val Lynch. A full brother to Clint, Wade "Huggy," and Jerry he was a junior in high school when the rodeo program was implemented. He was the oldest brother and leader of the flock.

I recently passed through the city in New Mexico Val now calls home and gave him a call. He dropped by my motel after work, wearing a company shirt. I hadn't seen him since his mother's funeral six years earlier. Before that, a dozen years had gone by since we'd visited at Clint's funeral.

Seeing him brought back more vivid memories for me. We had some good laughs along with some sobering moments as he shared things I had never known before. Wade had once

GLEN TERRY   NORTH SANPETE H.S, RODEO   MANTI 1977

told me how Val, a blue-eyed kid with plastic-frame glasses and light brown hair, had been small for his age in junior high and had taken a lot of grief because of his stature, weighing in at a mere 120 pounds. Apparently he would only take so much, though, because he'd often ended up with a black eye and a cracked lip.

On the first day of junior high, a much taller kid had started pushing Val around. That had upset Wade, and he'd made quick business of the entire thing by pushing the kid into the coat rack. According to Val, Wade had the worst temper of any of the brothers and was also the most bullheaded.

"I sure remember that day," Val told me. "We all ended up in the principal's office. The office called our mother. Mom was slow to anger, but when you got her mad, she was *mad.*

As the door to the principal's office opened, we could hear our mother's voice. Her visit changed the way we were treated."

When I first met Wade, he was a member of the high school wrestling team. Tipping the scales at 160, he was known as "Huggy," the guy who could "back a bull dog out of a meat locker." The nickname had been given to him in junior high. Though Val also wrestled in high school, he hadn't tipped the scales at nearly the number his brother had: at five-foot-nine he still weighed around 120 pounds. But that didn't last long. He joined the National Guard in high school and came back from basic training weighing 165 and having gained two inches in height.

Val had also been in the music club at the high school, something that, as with his teammates, seemed to work in his favor when riding broncs. Val had also joined the high school tennis club during his sophomore year, but when high school rodeo became sanctioned as a club, Val put music and tennis on the back burner. He could see himself riding bucking horses and bulls much more easily than he could see himself playing tennis.

As we reminisced, Val reminded me of how poor his family had been. The house the boys had lived in was a small, white-framed house on State Street at the south end of town. It could have used a little paint, some repairs, and a few more furnishings. Their father died the day he met with a freak accident, when Val was nine, a day he vividly remembers. Their mother was a single parent who struggled to raise a family of five—including their only sister, Becky—on a mighty tight budget.

And although the family experienced some extremely tough times, they did have a couple of riding horses. The boys often rode their horses downtown to get groceries or to run other errands. At times they even parked their horses in the center of town at the Dairy Freez. Reflecting on those hard times, Val said, "I met the guy who was with my father six years earlier when he shot himself, and he told me what had really happened. Alcohol was the cause of everything bad that happened to our family. My father and this fellow were drunk. They had a pistol they thought was unloaded. As they played around with the gun, my father put the barrel in his mouth and pulled the trigger. For years everyone believed it was a suicide, but it was an accident." After a moment of silence, Val continued. "It was closed casket. My father's sister had them open it. She told us to give him a kiss. That was tough. Wade took it the hardest."

Could rodeo make a difference for all of these boys? I believed it could. Danny, Casey, Rusty, Glen, and Val began making North Sanpete High School Rodeo history in the spring of that school year. The SideKicks' first high school rodeo under the North Sanpete High School Rodeo Club banner had its beginnings in the red dirt of southeastern Utah. Would these boys be able to face their fears and come out wanting to do it over and over again? Would they escape serious injury? Would high school rodeo be worth the risk involved? Those questions pummeled my mind repeatedly as SideKicks adventure began.

CHAPTER SIX

The Excitement Begins

A Lesson Learned: Don't Be Afraid When Opportunity Knocks

OUR FIRST high school rodeo was in April 1976. I felt a tremendous weight of responsibility on my shoulders; there was always the possibility of injury, but I didn't want to think about that at a time when I was encouraging my students to look fear in the eye. The excitement of the students helped lighten my load. We found ourselves getting pumped up for a new high school experience and looking forward with great anticipation to the trip to Moab. It would turn out to be a unique journey for North Sanpete High.

The previous school day proved fruitless for the five Side-Kicks. Not one of them could concentrate on anything but what awaited them in Moab. We were now able to relate to what football players and their coaches went through before a game. Adding to their excitement was the chance to get out of school for a few days.

Danny, a junior that year, volunteered to take his pickup—a 1965 Chevrolet blue half-ton 327 built to the max. I planned on taking my small 1974 Chevy two-tone brown station wagon as our other vehicle. The other North Sanpete rodeo players— Casey, Val, Shorty, and Rusty—were full of anticipation. Their feet were barely touching the ground. The school district was paying for lodging and meals; without that support, the trip would have been a financial burden to the students.

The SideKicks piled into my station wagon and Danny's truck, tossing their rodeo bags in the back of the pickup, and we started the five-hour drive to Moab. Traveling between Salina and Green River, my loaded station wagon, with its gas-saving engine, was struggling to climb some of the hills. At one point as I was dragging along at forty miles an hour with the pedal to the metal going uphill, I suddenly felt a push. In my rearview mirror I saw Danny with his truck against my rear bumper and a smile on his face. As the bumpers grated against each other, my car started to fishtail. It occurred to me then that the most dangerous part of the trip wasn't going to be riding stock but Danny's driving.

Upon our safe arrival, we checked into our motel and grabbed a bite to eat. Afterward, we went to our rooms—I had my own, and the five cowboys shared another. As things settled down, it felt good to get a little shuteye.

At 3:00 a.m., I began reliving my first bareback bronc-riding experience. Before I continue, though, I'd probably better give a little information about the two types of bronc riding. Saddle and bareback bronc riding are significantly different. With the first, the rider uses a saddle that consists of stirrups but no horn. The rider holds on to a braided rein, trying to spur the horse forward and backward with his feet from over the point of the horse's shoulder to the cantle in a rhythm. The greater the distance covered, the higher he can score points. The bareback rider, on the other hand, uses no saddle. Back in the day, he held on to a rigging made of hard, toughened leather that was placed upon the animal's withers. These days the rigging is made of fiberglass, metal, and rawhide and is as tough as can be. As opposed to the saddle bronc rider's motion, the bareback rider rakes his spurs from the point of the shoulder of the bronc up toward the handle of his rigging, finding a rhythm with each of the horse's jumps.

Back in the day, I was a member of Snow College's rodeo club, and we had acquired some practice broncs. With the help of half a dozen club members, I climbed onto the back of one of those critters in the bucking chute. As I lowered myself onto the horse, I started to wonder if it was a smart thing for me to be doing. I was shaking in my boots. I wanted to have the experience, but I also wanted to live.

When they opened the gate, all hell broke loose. My bronc reared up and leaped forward, then his front feet came down as he lunged forward yet again. A jerk ripped through my entire body as those front feet hit the ground that second time. My legs were somewhere on the bronc's neck, and I felt totally out of control as he continued his forward motion. I knew I should be doing something with my legs, but my thoughts were on my hands and on trying to hang on for dear life. I continued the ride much like a dummy; in fact, I felt like a dummy just being in that situation.

I went to what my father had taught me while riding colts out on our plowed ground. I could hear him yelling, "Hang on! Hang on!" as the colts bucked. I gave it my best effort through a couple more jumps, just hanging on. As I hit the ground, I felt an adrenaline rush, but mostly I just felt grateful to be alive.

As I sat there in the middle of the arena, I watched my bronc jump over the fence, run through the gate, and gallop off down Highway 89. As he ran toward downtown Ephraim, I was glad to be sitting there in the dirt instead of on his back. I had gotten off pretty easy. My teeth had sliced my upper lip and I was bleeding, but it could've been much worse. What an adventure that had been. As I drifted back into a restless sleep, I wondered what the next day would hold for the SideKicks.

* * *

The excitement was palpable as we got into our automobiles and headed to the rodeo grounds that morning. On arrival, we could hear the sound system putting out country music. There were cowboys and cowgirls everywhere, and you could feel the electricity in the air.

We were about to make North Sanpete High School history in Moab. I had to pinch myself to see if all of it was real and not just a dream.

The SideKicks got their riggings and bull ropes ready. You could hear the ripping of athletic tape as arms were being taped. Bareback bronc riders began working rosin into their riding gloves and into the handles of their bareback rigging. Bull riders tied their bull ropes off on a top rail and rubbed rock rosin into them, which afforded a better grip. I could imagine the boys visualizing their rides and courageously battling their fears as they prepared their riding equipment. Every once in a while a joke, a sigh, or burst of laughter would break the tension.

As the bucking horses were being loaded into the chutes, the announcer began to talk and the rodeo came alive. After the grand entry and introductions, the cowboys and cowgirls respectfully removed their hats for the national anthem. Then everything went suddenly quiet as the announcer read "A Cowboy's Prayer."

Val Lynch on Roan Light, UHSRA Finals, Heber City, 1977

After the prayer, the bareback bronc riding began. Danny began pacing back and forth in front of the bucking chutes. I tried to imagine what was going through his mind; he looked as nervous as I'd felt when he'd given me a push with his truck. I couldn't help but notice the ambulance parked by the gate to the arena.

It was time for Danny to climb down onto the back of his bronc. I was relieved to see his horse behaving in the chute; those not behaving generally made for rattled nerves, especially for a beginner. I could imagine what Danny was feeling. His first bareback bronc-riding experience. Once you were on that horse's back gripping the handhold of your rigging, you realized that a nod of your hat would start what was guaranteed to be an adrenaline rush like no other. Suddenly things would get out of control, and you'd begin to think the only way you could get out of it was a nosedive into the dirt. As that didn't sound much fun, you hung on until the choice was no longer yours. Then, lying in the dirt, you realized you've survived, and a good feeling suddenly washed over you.

Danny took the time to get a good grip on the handle of his bareback rigging, then got in position to be "tapped out"— with his legs up on the shoulders of his bronc so he could get his heels over the horse's shoulder on that first jump out of the chute. Then Danny nodded his head, and the gate flew open.

It was a mighty bumpy ride. I was sure he'd never experienced anything quite like it. Danny used every bit of strength he could muster, but his legs ended up all over the place and out of control—his right leg high, his left low. He continued to lean back and hang on, though, gritting his teeth and probably wondering how he'd got himself into a situation like this.

When they reached the middle of the arena, the horse kicked into the air with his back feet and Danny went up. We watched as gravity slammed him into the red dirt. Then the whistle blew. As Danny picked himself up and walked back to the chutes, there was a smile on his face and the unmistakable expression that adrenalin brings.

Up next, Casey climbed down onto Starburst. I experienced an instant rerun of nerves as he settled on his bronc; I wondered if Casey would have preferred to be back in school sitting at a desk instead of on the back of a horse about to explode into action. I knew his body was vibrating, his heart pounding, and every muscle in his body becoming taut.

Casey nodded his head, the gate opened, and his hand was suddenly full of horsepower. His bronc jumped out of that chute, first rearing up and then suddenly dropping, then doing it again and again while Casey put forth his best effort to hang on.

When I saw daylight between him and his horse, I knew Casey was at the end of his ride. Suddenly he flew into the air and, before he knew it, had hit the dirt and had the air knocked out of him, but he returned to the chutes with a smile on his face, a pick-up man by his side to see him safely back. You gotta love those guys who come to a rider's rescue once his time is up.

Casey recently told me, "That bronc ride in Moab was a first; I had ridden some sheep and calves when I was a younger but nothing like that. Since then, I have done some sky diving, and the same thoughts entered my mind: *Should I even be doing this? Well, it's too late to back out now.* Then came the butterflies, followed by the adrenalin rush." He continued, "I didn't stay on very long, and when I hit the arena floor, I hurt. I also remember emptying red dirt out of my boots. But we sure did have fun in Moab that weekend, didn't we?"

Next it was Val's turn to face his fears; he drew a bronc by the name of Blue Rocket. As Val began to climb down onto the back of that animal, the horse stood there like he'd been broken to ride. What a relief; the horse's calm allowed Val to stay focused on more important things.

When Val nodded and the gate opened, Blue Rocket suddenly acted like he had just run into a wasp nest. I watched as Val tried his best to hang on; it wasn't a pretty ride, but the kid displayed true grit and determination. He later described it as a mixture of excitement and fright followed by an amazing adrenalin rush.

"As I slid up to my rigging and called for the gate," he said, "I thought, *This is the craziest thing I have ever done. I hope I survive this trip.* When I hit the ground, I thought, *What a rush!* I couldn't wait to get on another bronc."

Val had actually ridden the horse for the full eight seconds, then ended up face-first in the dirt. He wasn't aware that a pick-up man was available to put him down on the ground more gently. Sadly, he'd failed to mark out his horse at the chute and ended up with a no-score. ("Marking out" means a rider should have the spurs on his boots in contact with the horse over the point of the shoulders before the horse's front legs hit the ground.)

The last event in Moab was bull riding. With a whole new sense of anticipation, we watched as Rusty and Shorty finished rubbing the dry rosin into their bull ropes and their bulls were loaded into the chute. The bull rope is the main piece of equipment for this event. It's a rope with leather braided into the handle for extra strength. A strip of leather is braided into the bull rope to add strength and wear to the rope. One end of the rope is tied in a knot so that the rope can be adjusted to fit around different sized bulls. The other end, or what we call the tail, is a flat braid coated with rosin for a good grip. Once the bull is in the chute, it's time to put the rope around the animal, a loop in one end of the rope. Someone reaches under the bull with a wire hook and brings the loop to the side. The other end of the rope is taken through the loop and tied off until it's time to mount.

Rusty drew a Scotch Highlander bull named Scotty, owned by Larry Russell of the Rockin' R Rodeo Company. Red in color and while not extremely big, Scotty had a set of horns that looked long and dangerous—the kind you wouldn't want to get too close to. His hair was so long that Rusty had to pull it out from under the bull rope before they could get it in place.

Rusty climbed on the back of his bull, resting his feet on the sides of the chute, and made the final adjustments to his bull rope. Tightening his grip, he gave his clenched fist a couple of good hits with his other hand to assure a solid hold. When he nodded, his bull lunged forward as the gate opened and caught his horn on the chute, giving Rusty the option for a reride on another bull with a new start out the gate. Rusty quickly nodded yes, and the handlers got a new bull in the chute.

Shorty helped Rusty pull his bull rope again after Rusty took his seat and put his hand into the braided handle of his rope. With a few quick jerks, Shorty and Rusty drew the rope tight. The bull snorted as Rusty wrapped the rope around the back of his hand and then through his open fist. He clenched his fist tight. Ready, he nodded, and the gate flew open. Rusty's bull literally came out of that chute on a roll, carrying on like a crazy tiger. After a few good jumps, Rusty was off that bull faster than a "car-wash minute."

The final SideKick to ride in Moab that weekend was Shorty. When he climbed down on Rawhide, his rope was already wrapped around the animal and tied off. The flank man had also tied the flank strap loosely around the bull's flanks. Shorty appeared to have little fear as he sat carefully on his bull and began heating up the rosin on his rope with his riding glove. Rusty pulled Shorty's bull rope snug, then together the boys gave it an extra tug to make sure it was drawn tight around the bull's belly. Shorty reached for the tail of his rope with his opposite hand, brought it into his glove, and wrapped it around the back of his hand, leaving a little bubble on the back side of his hand—something he'd been told to do with this particular bull.

Leaning slightly forward, he nodded for the gate to open. The stock contractor quickly pulled the flank strap snug as they left the chute. When Shorty's bull made its first leap into the

Rusty Bench   UHSRA Finals   Heber City   1977

arena, Shorty felt the bubble tighten around his hand as the beast's gut expanded.

Shorty appeared tougher than his cowboy boots as he sat glued to Rawhide's back. The bull rapidly moved first to the right and then to the left and then to the right again, twisting and bucking the whole time. Shorty hung on for a full four seconds, but then his hips shifted and he started to go off the left side. It appeared this would be his trip to the dirt, but he somehow made a remarkable comeback. His ride continued for another five, six, seven, and finally eight full seconds! An eternity for a bull ride. As the whistle blew, Shorty hit the dirt and the bull went on his way down the arena. Shorty placed fifth in bull riding that weekend in Moab, giving us some success to take home.

The conversation centered on our experiences in Moab as we made our way back to the school. The level of excitement was much higher coming home than it had been going. Though Shorty's fifth-place win in bull riding was the icing on the cake, we knew the trip to Moab was not all about winning—it was about having fun, which we'd accomplished in spades.

Monday morning, the boys' classmates were excited to hear all about Moab and seemed a little surprised no one had been injured. As the others gather around, the weekend adventures were repeated and the experiences relived. All of the SideKicks beamed as they walked the halls of North Sanpete that week, heads held a little higher. It was obvious other club members were inspired by what the five SideKicks had just experienced in Moab.

When I think about that first competition, what remains foremost in my mind is the boys' courage. It takes pure grit for a high school student to sit on the back of a bronc or bull for the first time. Knowing you could be tossed high in the air or injured by a manic animal after getting dumped can rattle anyone's nerves. Anyone with a pulse would certainly feel fear. But the payoff at Moab had been phenomenal. Some of those SideKicks had been ready to give up on school when I arrived at North Sanpete High School. These same students were now energized and seemed to have a new outlook on life.

Being on the football and/or basketball team opened doors for certain students, but membership on those teams was limited, for obvious reasons. Before the rodeo club, other students could have those kinds of experiences only in their dreams. Now these students realized that there were also doors open for them and wonderful experiences to be had through high school sports. And there was plenty of talk about the natural highs that had come as they'd faced their fears in Moab.

CHAPTER SEVEN

Adventures Continue

A Lesson Learned: Never Allow Setbacks to Keep You from Reaching Your Dream

AND TALK ABOUT facing your fears and overcoming trials. Brothers Casey and John Larsen sure rose to the occasion in this respect. When John was six years old and Casey four, their mother passed away from a rare type of cancer similar to that which had taken the life of world champion bareback rider Chris Ledoux. When they later told me of their mother's passing, I thought of world champion bull rider Donny Gay losing his mother to leukemia when he was three. Their stories seemed pretty similar. Because they'd lost Mom so young, the Larsen boys had grown up without much coddling and learned early on how to take care of themselves.

When it came time for high school rodeo, the Larsen brothers had their father's support. Rex was a bareback bronc rider and a member of the Professional Rodeo Cowboys Association. It was rough, I'm sure, for John and Casey to stay in school while their peers were in Moab participating in a high school rodeo. Apparently, John and Casey had not only been short on funds but on parent signatures as well since their father had been away herding sheep to provide for the boys and their sisters.

As a sheepherder, Rex spent most of his time away from home—out on the desert during the winter months and on the mountain ranges in the summer. When he did come home, the boys told me, he expected a clean camp. If things weren't clean, they got a boot kick. Nonetheless, both boys respected their father, who took care of his family as best he could. He left an open account at the local grocery store so they could get groceries and other things they needed; he even left money for them to wash their clothes.

"Our father never questioned our charges, and we never gave him reason to be concerned," Casey said. "My father rode broncs and bulls in pro rodeo until he was fifty-two years old. I never remember him being thrown off a bronc horse. At times his rides would get a little sloppy, but he always managed to get off with the help of a pick-up man."

School had been pretty uneventful for the Larsen brothers— that is, until high school rodeo came along. Then things began to change, sometimes for the better and sometimes for the worst.The second high school rodeo of the season was held in Pleasant Grove. John and Casey had both entered, wanting to find out what they had missed in Moab. Casey had drawn out in the bareback bronc riding event, while John was going to ride a bull.

Casey drew a bronc named Nevada Boy, a horse owned by Circle J Rodeos. As Casey climbed down on him, he carefully eased himself up close to his rigging. Getting a good handhold on the handle, he leaned back, tucked his chin, gritted his teeth, lifted on his rigging, and nodded for the gate. When the gate opened, Nevada Boy momentarily stalled in the chute as he took a look out in the arena, long enough for Casey to get a "free roll" (granted by the judge when a horse stalls for some time, meaning the rider doesn't need to "mark him out" to earn points).

BLAKE NIELSEN "BUCKWHEAT" NORTH SANPETE H.S. RODEO MANTI 1977

When someone finally pushed the horse's neck, he just plain knocked it out of neutral. Nevada Boy blew into that arena bucking first to the right and then to the left; it was difficult to tell which direction he was going next. Casey continued to go with him one jump at a time, keeping his eyes riveted to Nevada Boy's neck, figuring that wherever that horse's neck went, the horse's body would follow.

Casey stayed on Nevada Boy until the horse hit a cameraman. Then he apparently lost his concentration and ended up in the air. Getting up on his feet after a rather rough landing, he glanced back at the cameraman. As he headed back to the chute, he said, "I ran into a little bad luck on that one, but I'm sure glad neither of us got hurt."

When it was John's turn, I wondered who was more excited. He climbed down on the back of Bob Cat, a bull with a set of horns that looked like they could cause pain. His riding glove on his right hand, John began heating up the rosin. My heart started to beat faster as I watched him adjust his bull rope so the handhold was in the right spot, then put his hand in that built-in slot of his bull rope, his little finger lining up just slightly to the right of Bob Cat's backbone. Taking the wrap behind his hand, he ran the rope through it and closed it tight, flipping the tail of his bull rope over the bull's hump as he scooted up to the rope.

I could hear one of John's buddies telling him what to do, giving him some last-minute instructions on how to ride a bull. John didn't seem to be listening. He had other things on his mind as he called for the gate to open with the nod of his hat.

In a flash, Bob Cat came out of the chute and went airborne, doing a twist and then a turn in rapid-fire succession. Almost two tons of bull yanked on John's arm as he went wherever that bull wanted to take him. As he hung on, John tried to anticipate the moves of the bull, staying square, focused, and in the middle of the bull's back. His goal was to ride Bob Cat for eight seconds and then escape before the bull got him with those horns—or, even worse, with his hooves. I could only imagine the damage an 1,800-pound bull could do as those feet came down on a rider. A bronc usually tries to avoid stepping on his rider—not so with a bull.

John managed to stay in the middle, even up on his rope for the first three jumps. But with the fourth jump, things started to change. As the bull turned back into his hand, John, not having a countermove in place, got back on his rope at the same time as his feet popped up. When he lost his feet, he lost his seat. That bull bumped him right out the back door.

John landed right where that bull could've nailed him real good with his horns and then stomped him with his feet. But just in the nick of time, the rodeo clowns were there to divert the bull's attention. With a rush of adrenalin, John sprinted back to the bucking chutes. With a smile on his face, we heard him say, "I had that bull rode, then someone opened the gate." It was obvious he was feeling good. He had looked fear square in the eye without even blinking.

I was relieved that we had not sustained any injuries. Instead, we took home some never-to-be-forgotten memories from Pleasant Grove that weekend. As the advisor, I had hoped to see an eight-second ride. What I saw instead were two high school students who were now excited about school and about life. Their experiences in Pleasant Grove seemed to open up a whole new vision of self-worth, self-confidence, and a greater hold on life.

* * *

John's next rodeo would be in Price. He was joined by fellow SideKicks Tim Larsen and Dale Peel, who both enjoyed the thrill of riding bulls. Tim was Casey and John's cousin; their fathers were brothers. The trip was one the boys would remember for the rest of their lives. Dale described his bull ride as "brief," which was apt—either at the nod of his hat or as the bull left the chute, Dale and that bull parted company.

That's definitely not what happened to John—he and his bull refused to part company, even after the sound of the whistle. John was still solidly planted on that bull until he suddenly lost his seat and things took a turn for the worse. As John was thrown off the bull, his riding hand got stuck in his bull rope.

That's when things got real ugly. The bull went into a spin, whipping John around like a ragdoll. Trying to stay close to the side of the bull, John did his best to stay on his feet.

Seconds seemed more like minutes as the rodeo clowns and even the stock contractor jumped in to try to release John's hand from the bull rope. The bullfighters also got into the fray, trying to grab the tail of the rope. But the more they tried, the more they got hammered, the bull doing a fair share of damage.

The bull flinging John around likely weighed more than four defensive NFL linemen—and the power in just one stomp could be several times greater than a line drive from a major league baseball hitter. For those of us watching, those suspense-filled seconds got our hearts pounding and our adrenalin surging.

Tim later summed it up. "That was the worst hang-up I had ever seen. That bull simply wore himself out dragging John around—first in a little circle, then in increasingly larger circles. When the bull stepped on John's legs, it finally pulled John away from his bull rope. By that time the bull was tired, John's legs were torn up, and the two bullfighters and the stock contractor were also injured. It was a ride that went from bad to ugly."

All four ended up in the hospital; the stock contractor had the most severe injuries. Dale drove John to the hospital; fortunately, he had insurance through his high school rodeo membership. He didn't have any broken bones but he was one sore, bruised-up bull rider.

Doubts started rushing into my mind. Had I stayed in Las Vegas and not started the Rodeo Club, John might not have had such an ugly experience. Those who'd tried to help him might not have ended up in the hospital. But then I realized all the things they would have missed.

Dale remembers, "That night I threw my sleeping bag out in a plowed furrow and spent the night under the stars. Wherever John spent the night, I'm sure he was not very comfortable." Kelly Poulsen was another SideKick who competed in Price. He and a couple other SideKicks went to visit John at the hospital. As he told it, "We found him in a wheelchair in a room all by himself. John said, 'They have just left me here right next to that dead person covered up with a blanket. Get me out of here!' We found his clothes, threw them onto the wheelchair, put his hat on his head, and headed down the hall and out the door. We loaded him in the truck, and back to the arena we went."

Whenever there were dark clouds, however, there always seemed to be a silver lining somewhere, if you looked for it. Kelly recalled an experience they had on the way to the rodeo: "Our truck broke down right at the top of the mountain. We had our bedrolls with us and were planning to spend the night; we were so poor back then we couldn't afford a motel room. A married couple came by and stopped to lend us a hand. After helping us get our truck running, they told us we were *not* sleeping there. At their invitation, we followed them, and they put us up in their home for the night in a nice, comfortable bed. They even fed us breakfast the next morning. The only thing we could figure was that they liked people wearing cowboy hats."

Still, I wondered if that infamous hang-up would be the end of John's bull-riding career. The fact that his dad had competed in professional rodeos until he was fifty-two indicated there was a degree of toughness in John's heritage. John had also been part of that group who'd ridden their horses forty miles over the mountain to attend the rodeo in Huntington. John was a tough kid, but to get dragged around like a popper on the end of a bullwhip could make even a tough SideKick rethink this rough-stock adventure through more carefully.

* * *

In Ogden, Casey Larsen took another wild ride on a horse named Yellow Fever. That horse was bad even in the chute; they'd had to tie his head so he wouldn't rear up and pin Casey to the back wall. Bad accidents happened in bucking chutes, and Casey knew it. To his credit, he remained coolheaded as he climbed down onto his bronc, carefully placing his right hand into the handle of his rigging and easing himself up onto the handle of his rigging while holding on to the chute with his other hand. As he put his legs up to the shoulders of the horse, he knew he had to be careful not to touch the horse with his spurs or avoid any quick moves or noises—he was sitting on a virtual keg of dynamite.

His feet in place, Casey leaned back and nodded for the gate. "I finally got out on that bronc," Casey said. "When he came out of the chute, I rode him for almost the full eight seconds. Then I became momentarily hung up in my rigging handle as I was thrown into the air."

It ended up being an unbelievably rough night for Casey and his family. He spent the night in the hospital with a broken arm, and that same night his two sisters were injured in a car accident in Salt Lake City. After his father had done what he could for his two daughters, he picked Casey up from the hospital the next day and took him home.

In spite of all that happened to him in his first year of high school rodeo, unbelievably, Casey summarized it with enthusiasm: "I drew a bareback bronc horse named Oatis, rode him for eight seconds, and cracked my wrist. In Nephi, I drew a bareback horse named Dirty Sally, and I covered her for eight seconds. I was disqualified on a horse named Bay Rum because I touched him with my free arm. Then, in Price—my last rodeo during that first year—I drew a horse named Red Risk. I rode him for another eight seconds. I had ridden every one of those broncs, but I didn't place on any of them."

He had what was possibly his worst experience in Hurricane. According to Casey, "Reed, Tim, John, and I rode down to Hurricane in Reed's car. John and I drew out the first night of rodeo, where I got Blue Rocket. Then we went to the café, where I joked about ordering lizard soup. After we ate, we drove to the rodeo grounds. As I got my riggin' ready, I watched the horses being loaded into the bucking chutes. I could see that my draw was a bad chute fighter. Rusty and Kelly helped me down on my horse; he kept trying to buck the whole time he was in the chute. Finally, I got my hand in the riggin' and called for him.

"About three jumps out of the chute, he threw me right up over his rear end; on my way down he caught me right in the back of the head with his hoof. I did a couple of summersaults before I hit the ground. I stood up but fell right back down to my knees."

Someone waved the ambulance to come into the arena, and it pulled up right next to Casey. As they were loading him in, John ran over; out of breath, he gasped, "Wait—I'm up next, and I need his spurs."

I helped John wrestle the spurs off Casey's feet, examining them before giving them to John. Their father must have worn them during his pro rodeo days—they were the real deal. They had an shank offset at about fifteen degrees with small, dull rowels that would not cut into the horse's flesh but just sort of tickle the horse as they rolled along its neck.

I watched as the medics loaded Casey into the ambulance and then as the ambulance left the arena. Climbing into my own vehicle, I headed for the hospital in St. George, assuming that was where they would be taking Casey. But Casey had not been admitted. I drove back to the arena, but Casey wasn't there either. I finally headed to his motel room, and there he was—seemingly okay.

Rusty told me what had happened. "They took Casey in the ambulance and doctored him outside the arena. Then I took Casey to our motel room. The paramedics had told us to ask him his name, where he lived, and a few other questions just to make sure he did not have a concussion. Casey soon caught on to what we were doing and began giving us wrong answers. That's when we realized he was going to be okay."

The next morning, we met at the arena, where I was told that some other cowboys had come to Casey's room that evening after I'd left. They'd played poker until three in the morning while Casey lay in bed recuperating! We all felt lucky that Casey's injuries weren't worse than they were. Tim said, "From the kick of that bronc, it wouldn't have surprised anyone if Casey had died right there in the arena. That horse hoof against his head was like walking into a baseball bat. It showed all of us how tough Casey really was."

It wasn't long before Casey found himself on another bronc in the same arena during another rodeo. This bronc was an ornery, wiry critter not "user friendly" at all, but he was skinny enough to leave a little extra room for Casey to get his feet into starting position while in the chute. As Casey put his hand into his rigging, I noticed the small withers on his bronc.

I could see that Casey's adrenalin had started to flow. It had to be pumping hard when they opened that gate. The bronc entered the arena cranking wildly, wanting to get Casey off its back as quick as possible. But Casey did not want to get off—not yet, at least—which created a conflict between man and horse.

Casey picked up his timing after tapping, or marking, his bronc out. He'd made extra sure the heels of his boots were over his horse's shoulders on that first jump out. His bronc covered some ground as he jumped, kicked, hopped, and dropped; then, suddenly, it stopped hard and Casey flew forward, right over the dashboard, with his hand still in the handle of his rigging. The bronc then ducked back, turned, and went the opposite direction, leaving Casey sitting in the dirt with his hand still in the handle.

I could not believe what I was seeing. Casey was up on his feet, still holding the rigging with the cinch tied off. It appeared he had just performed some sort of magic as he strutted back to the chutes with a smile on his face. Casey had ridden that rigging right up over the withers of his bronc, which had then ducked out of Casey's bareback rigging. Incidentally, with the newer, more advanced riggings used today, that would have never happened. Today's riggings, as mentioned earlier, are much stiffer and more secure.

What it all boiled down to was this: Casey was tough as nails when it came be being an athlete. He had the makings of his father and grandfather when it came to riding broncs—a cowboy who could certainly be considered a chip off the old block.

Living a Dream

A Lesson Learned: Satisfaction Comes from Following Your Dreams

CONSIDERING THE INJURIES, disappointments, and hard knocks, you'd think at least some of the SideKicks would have lost interest in rodeo and called it quits. But they had found a new passion in their lives, they had experienced natural highs, and they were not about to let it go. And that meant they had to try harder in school to get passing grades so they could continue to participate in high school rodeo and follow their dreams.

One North Sanpete student—who was not a member of any of the clubs at the school—tried to hang himself in his bedroom; fortunately a family member saved him. I could only second-guess why he had wanted to take his own life. Maybe he was depressed, didn't feel he belonged, or didn't have any natural highs in his life. We may never know why. But I did know this: when I heard that news, high school rodeo injuries and hang-ups became much less of a concern to me.

One of the SideKicks, Robert Draper, had been reared in a humble environment, and school had not been one of his favorite places to hang out. I watched as he hobbled around school with crutches after having broken his leg while riding a horse at his place. Shorty told me Robert had purchased one mean burro. He would charge anyone who even threw a hat at him. When he bucked, it was with his head in the air, so the rider had to keep a real short buck rein to ride him. Shorty said, "That was the only saddle bronc I ever rode, and it was a jackass."

That burro seemed to have been a real confidence-builder for Robert, though. As soon as he had his cast removed, he approached me at school and said, "I want to enter the saddle bronc event at the Juab High School Rodeo in Nephi."

"Are you sure?" I asked. "You just got your leg out of a cast."

"I'm sure," he said. "My leg feels a lot better on a horse than in a cast."

My first instinct was to refuse, but then my mind went to the student who had tried to hang himself, and I thought, *If this is what Robert needs to make life more enjoyable, let him enter. Who was I to stop Robert from living his dream?*

And so I let Robert go ahead and enter. Those first attempts always made me a little uneasy, regardless of who the rider was. Things could quickly get out of control on these first rides, much like a teenager driving a racecar for the first time. Often it was a green cowboy just hanging on for dear life. And when that cowboy hit the ground, I often held my breath until he started walking back to the chute and I knew he wasn't injured.

I got chills thinking about how the average bucking horse weighed as much as five pro football defensive linemen. That's a lot of power in a horse that is out of control. Robert and I had both placed stock saddles on riding horses, but we had never before put a bronc saddle on a bronc. As I began helping Robert place that saddle on his bronc, he asked, "Is this the right spot?"

"I'm not sure," I told him. "This is a first for me too."

About that time, a local, seasoned saddle bronc rider I knew walked passed us. I asked Sam if he'd give us a hand. He took

GLEN TERRY "SILVER DOLLAR" NORTH SANPETE H.S. RODEO - MANTI 1977

the bronc saddle and placed it higher up on the withers than we had. He then helped Robert measure his buck rein correctly.

The next thing I knew, the announcer said, "Our next bronc rider is Robert Draper, a member of the SideKicks." I held my breath as I watched the gate open. Robert's bronc left the chute in a rear-out motion, moving forward. Robert's spurs looked like they were over the point of the shoulder, at least from my side, when his bronc's feet first connected with the ground. Soon Robert was in the middle of the arena. That bronc really tried to get Robert off his back, but Robert refused to go. He stayed seated until the whistle blew, and then they parted company as quickly as a couple getting a divorce.

Robert had qualified with thirty-five points. Had he gotten his legs in rhythm with his bronc, he could have easily picked up an additional fifteen or twenty. When Robert walked out of the arena unassisted, I was elated. Robert had the potential to become a competitive saddle bronc rider in high school rodeo.

I was grateful we hadn't placed that bronc saddle where I thought it should go. Robert would have had a better view of Juab Valley while being thrown into space, but he would have missed the joy of staying seated until the whistle blew.

* * *

When Kelly Poulsen was young, the one thing he wanted to do was ride bulls and bucking horses. Joining SideKicks was a dream come true for Kelly. He once told me, "High school sports never really interested me, but I did like to keep myself in shape so that I was fit for high school rodeo. In fact, I became pretty good at skipping rope during PE. I could cross over and even skip on one foot with ease."

Kelly had joined the SideKicks from neighboring South Sanpete High. The son of a government trapper, he had spent a good part of his growing-up years outdoors with his father, living in a tent, enjoying pack trips in the mountains, and becoming a cowboy poet.

Kelly told me about one poem he wrote one day when riding after a snowstorm. "The trees and branches were still covered with snow. My friend Rick was riding a little white mule we had taken on many rides and pack trips before. I had always paid attention to this mule and his abilities, which were quite extraordinary.

"As we were riding along, I began reciting my poem. Rick said, 'Where did you hear that?' I said, 'I didn't hear it anywhere; I just made it up.' He told me to write it down, and I said, 'On what? Even the toilet paper is wet.'"

When they got back to camp that night, Kelly wrote down "Little White Mule":

He was short from his hooves to his knees.
And when I first saw him, and noticed his speed,
that's how his name Lightning came to be.
He had the color of the fresh white snow,
that laid in the meadows where he wintered,
and the nights got down to forty below.
We rode him in the foothills, the mountains,
and the ruffs. Now, I'm here to tell you,
the little white mule was tough.
For he always packed the heaviest of men,
and the heaviest of loads,
across those rocky trails,
never once did he stumble nor roll.
Won lots of bets from the home folks in town,
for the many good steeds
he put to the ground.
Now he wasn't mean for kicking,
nor did he ever buck.
He was easily caught each morning,
right after chuck.
So I thank my good fortune,
and luck, you see,
to know a little white mule,
called Lightning and him a partner.

Money was tight for that cowboy poet, so he worked for various farmers after school to earn enough money to purchase some rodeo gear. "I was on my way to the Hurricane High School rodeo with Shorty and Rusty," he told me. "We stopped at Burns Saddlery in Salina on the way. I purchased a brand-new pair of Tony Lama cowboy boots, a new shirt, and a new silver-belly, four-and-a-half-inch-brim cowboy hat."

The bareback bronc horse Kelly drew at that rodeo was mighty rank in the chute and had quite an attitude. While Kelly was trying to get on him, he turned his head around and grabbed the side of Kelly's new boot with his teeth, tearing a chunk of leather right out of it.

"I finally got myself situated and nodded for the gate," Kelly said. "I was determined to get even with him for what he had done to my new boot. As that horse aggressively jumped out of the chute, my new hat flew off my head. Once I was back on the ground, I picked up my hat only to see a four-inch cut right down the front side of the brim from when the pick-up man ran over it. I couldn't believe it. I hadn't owned my hat and boots for more than six hours, and I had bought them with hard-earned money.

"At least my new shirt was still in good shape. When I got home, I stitched the brim of my hat and patched my boot. I have since had many good laughs over that hat and boot. That memory has brought many years of enjoyment."

Talk began circulating among club members about riding saddle broncs. However, no one had access to a bronc saddle. Not many things stopped me, though—where there was a will, there was usually a way.

CHAPTER NINE

Bronc Saddle

A Lesson Learned: Setting a Goal Opens Doors to Opportunity

THE SIDEKICKS always bought action photos at the rodeos in which they were contestants, and they turned their favorites in to me, so I used the photos to make a calendar to be sold as a fund-raising project. With the profit from the calendars and other fund-raising activities, the SideKicks accumulated nearly $800. The club set a goal to raise enough to purchase a bronc saddle. It's amazing how things seem to fall in place when you're trying to help others succeed. We didn't realize how close that saddle really was.

The Snow College Rodeo Club sponsored a rough-stock school at Denton's Indoor Arena, which was just a few miles down the road from us. Shorty enrolled in the bull-riding portion of the seminar. He was among eighty-three enrollees who had come from Texas, New Mexico, Arizona, Nevada, California, Idaho, South Dakota, and Utah.

Shorty was excited. He seemed to be the "man of the day" as he strutted the halls of North Sanpete High School. I could understand why as I considered the credentials of the instructors under which he would learn. The saddle bronc instructor was Shawn Davis of Twin Falls, Idaho—a three-time world champion in saddle bronc competitions, an eleven-time National Finals

Rodeo qualifier, and a National Finals intercollegiate saddle bronc champion. Shawn had started saddle bronc riding in high school, something that gave Shorty hope.

The bareback bronc riding instructor was J. C. Trujillo of Prescott, Arizona. A national finalist, Trujillo would become the bareback bronc riding world champion in 1981.

But it was John Davis of Homedale, Idaho, who most excited Shorty. Davis was a four-time National Finals qualifier and the first man to ride the famous bull Oscar—and Shorty knew that making a qualified ride on Oscar was quite an accomplishment. Oscar had come out of the chute a hundred times without a bull rider making a qualified ride. Though weighing in at only 1,300 pounds, Oscar would spin violently to the left as he came out of the chute, leaving the rider scrambling for safety. Shorty was looking forward to becoming acquainted with the man who had ridden that bull to the sound of the buzzer.

After the seminar, Shorty talked about how he liked the school because the pros had helped him in his bull riding: "John Davis showed me how to sit on a bull, how to take my wraps with my rope, and how to keep my feet down and into the bull. But most of all, he built my confidence by telling me how good I looked riding bulls."

Shorty never got thrown while at the school. He even won the end-of-school contest and a scholarship to another bull-riding school. Best of all, he got the highest score riding a bull.

The instruction we received at that school was invaluable, its teachers true examples of what it took to be successful. Shawn Davis stressed the importance of lifting the buck rein to keep the rider down in the saddle and to prevent the spurs from getting snagged on the rein. At one point he came out on a saddle bronc only to get his spur snagged on his buck rein—and he was rapidly bucked off. A few snickers rippled through the observers as he picked himself up off the ground. With a smile on his face, he shook his head in disbelief. What an effective teaching moment for that instructor, and what a great learning moment for his students.

I never would have guessed that soon after that seminar I would run into Shawn Davis again in Denver—and that our meeting would help the SideKicks get our bronc saddle. I was attending a rough-stock safety seminar being held during the National Western Livestock Show and Rodeo. Several of the top-ranked PRCA rodeo rough-stock riders were there to give instruction on how to protect a rider from being injured.

Dennis Reiners, one of the nation's top saddle bronc riders at the time, demonstrated what to do when a bronc rider "popped a swell." The swells of a bronc saddle are more extended than those of a stock saddle, which enables a bronc rider to lock his thighs tightly under the swells to keep himself down in his saddle. If a rider's thigh pops out, that cowboy is on his way to being bucked off—thus increasing his chances of being injured. Reiners demonstrated how, when a rider's thigh did pop out, he could quickly turn his toes out and the thigh would lock back under the swell. Other pros continued to offer valuable safety instruction throughout the seminar. I was rewarded with invaluable insights I could bring back to the SideKicks.

After the seminar, I headed back to the airport. As I entered the terminal, I saw a lone pair of black bronc-riding boots in the middle of the floor; the owner wasn't anywhere in sight. The boots had a low and rather wide upper vamp, which I knew was designed to allow a cowboy's foot to come out of his boot quickly if it got caught in the stirrup while being bucked off. As I looked at those boots, I recalled seeing a bronc rider years earlier being dragged by his bucking horse for some distance at the Ute Stampede Rodeo in Nephi. After what seemed like forever, his foot was finally released from that stirrup. *He really could have used a pair of these boots,* I thought.

After some time, the owner of the boots finally came and picked them up. It was Shawn Davis. I followed him as we boarded that airplane together. Unbelievably, my assigned seat happened to be next to his as we traveled back to Salt Lake City. During that flight, we talked about his ride at the National Western Rodeo. He said he'd scored low because it was getting difficult to draw good horses anymore. Our conversation then led into bronc saddles. I mentioned that the SideKicks club wanted to purchase a bronc saddle, and he told me he had designed one with a saddle maker in Ogden, Utah. He gave me his phone number and told me to give him a call.

When I got home, I called, and he said he would come to the school. It was not long before he showed up with a saddle. And it had *NS SideKicks* engraved on the fenders. Called an "association saddle," it was designed to meet the Rodeo Cowboys Association guidelines. With a full sixteen-inch seat, a rider could sit deep, lock his thighs under its swells, turn out his toes, and extend his legs to reach over the shoulders of his bronc. We gathered around as he showed us how to adjust the stirrups to get the right fit. Finally, we had our own bronc saddle—one with everything we had hoped for and more. We gladly handed him a check for $750. Our goal reached, the door to opportunity was now wide open.

CHAPTER TEN

Shifting into High Gear

A Lesson Learned: Natural Highs Encourage Success

THAT SECOND high school rodeo season, the SideKicks shifted into second gear. We aimed for greater winning opportunities but still preserved the fun. Our excitement and enthusiasm continued to escalate as we represented the high school at almost every rodeo throughout the state and became considered some of the most challenging competitors in Utah.

SideKicks Jon Larsen and Tim Larsen—not related—found themselves in the spotlight. Jon's father had been my dentist before he'd passed away. Jon had attended South Sanpete High and lived in Ephraim.

Tim's early years were spent on the west side of Salt Lake City in what Tim described as a bad section of town. During his sophomore year, his father died and he moved in with his cousins, Casey and John Larsen. Their living quarters consisted of a rather small wood-frame house on the east end of town. Washing clothes required a trip to the Laundromat. Tim laughed as he said that they sometimes had to look for their cleanest dirty shirt to wear.

Both Jon and Tim had entered the bull-riding event, and the SideKicks' excitement was palpable as we headed for the Huntington arena. Jon had drawn a bull by the name of Whiskey

Road, a mouse-colored Brahma with down-turned horns and rumored to be a handful once the gate opened. Jon knew he was in for a real ride.

Tim had also drawn Whiskey Road; he would ride the bull on Saturday, while Jon would ride him on Friday.

On Friday, Tim watched carefully as Jon came out of the chute on their bull. When the animal entered the arena, it was obvious it knew how to kick with its back feet, which went up in the air and came down with a sudden jolt before it took a giant leap forward with a twist and a turn, bucking and kicking in rapid-fire succession for at least four full jumps. Whiskey Road then circled clockwise. Then the wound-up bull headed back toward the chute, exerting tremendous effort to get Jon off its back. But Jon refused to be thrown and held on for a full eight seconds. Once the whistle sounded, he quickly jumped off and got to a safe area.

Saturday quickly rolled around, and it was Tim's turn to ride Whiskey Road. Tim mentally pictured himself making the same ride as Jon. Sure enough, Whiskey Road followed the same pattern as the day before, exploding out of the chute from the get-go. Tim also stayed on the bull for a full eight seconds before making a clean getaway.

Tim and Jon had tied for first place riding the same bull. The win ended up in a coin toss for the buckle and trophy. Jon called heads and Tim called tails. When it landed, it was facing upward. Jon took the buckle and Tim the trophy, and two happy SideKicks headed home for a good night's sleep.

* * *

And the excitement continued as nine SideKicks participated in an open high school rodeo jackpot sponsored by Emery High School Rodeo Club in the Ferron arena. Because it was not an approved high school rodeo, the top three winners in each event at this rodeo couldn't qualify for the State Finals Rodeo. However, it provided practice, gave experience, and built self-confidence.

John's bad bull-riding experience in Price didn't stop him from getting on another bull in Ferron; it's the "cowboy way"— when you get bucked off, you get back on. His bull gave him third-place honors during the Friday performance. John was bucked off on the second night, while Shorty captured fifth place after both nights of riding bulls. Shane Walters, a half-Navajo boy we called "Chief," experienced his first saddle bronc ride at this high school rodeo jackpot.

* * *

After the first year, as the momentum continued to build, several girls joined the SideKicks. One of the first to join was Crystal Watson, a girl who was involved in several school programs, including the music and girls' athletics clubs. Crystal left a big imprint on high school rodeo. She was later killed in a head-on collision while traveling to Colorado to visit her sister, leaving behind a young family and husband.

A new member of the SideKicks that year, Jimmy Christensen, displayed pure grit and determination during his first attempt at bareback bronc riding. If you want to know how much pure grit it takes, especially for a first ride, imagine being in a truck with different sized tires going down a rocky riverbed at forty miles per hour. In other words, Jimmy endured a rough ride.

Jimmy found it difficult to get his feet up over the bronc's shoulders, let alone get his legs working in a raking motion in time with the moves of his horse. He managed to stay aboard for a full five seconds before he went airborne.

He also entered the team-roping event, partnering with Shorty. He was the header and Shorty the healer, riding Buck, an old family horse who had no buck left in him—or so we thought. In the heading box, Jimmy gave the nod, the chute gate opened, the steer ran out, and Jimmy swung his lariat loop right over the steer's horns. Taking a look back at Shorty, Jimmy saw that Buck apparently didn't like what he was being asked to do. Totally out of character, the horse left the heeling box bucking and continued to buck until Shorty was able to catch a leg. They both went home with fifth-place honors in team roping that day.

Though he mostly rode bareback broncs, Jimmy did ride a few bulls. In fact, he'd even earned the nickname "Rawhide" on one particular ride in the Mount Pleasant arena. A bull had left a gash on his forehead, and, as Jimmy was being examined, some cowboy quipped, "I see rawhide." After that, the name stuck.

Though we were in our second year, most of the boys were still in tough financial straits. Tim had drawn a flat little bucking bull who suddenly cranked it on when it got to the middle of the arena. Tim's bull rope broke, and Tim ended up in the dirt, his bull rope still in his hand. Without the money to buy his own equipment, Tim had borrowed the bull rope from his cousin John. Tim told me, "After that handle broke, it took me two years to get enough money together to purchase my own rodeo equipment. That was how poor I was." But the SideKicks were experiencing such confidence and pure, natural highs, that the sacrifices were worth it.

* * *

Rusty became the first member of the SideKicks to qualify for the State High School Rodeo Finals. He took a third-place honor at Hurricane High School in saddle bronc riding, and contestants placing first, second, or third in a qualified high school rodeo were invited to participate at the state finals. Those placing first, second, third, or fourth at the Utah State Finals Rodeo received an all-expense-paid trip to the National High School Finals Rodeo.

Robert Draper became the second SideKick to qualify for state. He took a second-place win in saddle bronc riding that year. The club now had two chances to qualify for the National Rodeo Finals that year in Helena, Montana, from August 15 to the 21.

* * *

The SideKicks members were a determined lot despite any setbacks they encountered. At the Sevier High School Rodeo in Richfield, Val had climbed down on a bareback bronc, put his feet up tight against the shoulders of the horse, lifted the handle of his rigging, and tucked his chin down tight against his chest. He then nodded for the gate. As it opened, Val quickly placed his heels over the point of his bronc's shoulders and tapped him with his spurs.

His bronc hopped, twisted, kicked, and bucked, trying everything it could to get Val off its back, but Val hung on until the whistle. Though he'd made a qualified ride, his reward was a no-score. The judges claimed he had touched his bronc with his free arm while trying to stay on.

We had an unforgettable adventure in Richfield when Kevin Thompson entered the bareback bronc-riding competition. It was a first for Kevin. His parents were not supportive but had finally given written consent, I figured maybe because we were related—our grandfathers were brothers. As Kevin got down on his animal, it was obvious he had butterflies. We both wondered how this nerve-racking trip would end.

As soon as the gate opened, things became intense. Kevin's bronc popped the clutch and bolted out of the chute. Almost as soon as it started bucking, Kevin took a dive. As Kevin scrambled to his feet, I felt relieved when he appeared to be okay. But it wasn't over. As Kevin walked along the arena fence on his way back to the chute, the bronc suddenly started running toward him. "Watch out!" someone yelled. Kevin looked back, then hurriedly reached for a top rail and climbed onto the fence, narrowly avoiding what could've been a disaster.

Back behind the bucking chutes, John helped Kevin remove the elastic wrap from his riding arm. Once the wrap was removed, it was obvious Kevin had broken his arm; his hand just drooped. Kevin hadn't known the arm was broken until he'd reached for the top rung of the fence and climbed out of the way of the bronc. He was taken to the local hospital.

I drove Kevin home after the rodeo and walked into the house with him. I thought I'd better smooth things over with his mother the best I could. I hoped the family connection might help, but she took one look at Kevin's arm and then shot me a distraught and angry look.

"Now see what you have done!" she cried.

I got the distinct feeling she would have preferred I had stayed in Las Vegas.

At school the next day, Kevin's cast attracted lots of attention. Classmates gathered around to sign their autographs. Teachers even gave him favors. Not only was his cast on his riding arm, it was also on his writing arm—something that made the other students wish for a similar break (no pun intended). Unfortunately, that was the end of Kevin's bareback bronc riding in high school; his mother refused to sign any more permission slips for him.

Richard Rigby was at the same rodeo and was getting ready to climb down on his bull when they stopped the rodeo to attend to Kevin. Richard's bull began to act up in the chute, causing his nerves to rattle. As he attempted to take his seat, the bull shoved its horns hard against Richard's chest. When they opened the gate, it was about four good jumps and a fast getaway.

Val got ready for his first saddle bronc ride at this same rodeo. He'd taken a good, deep seat in the club's bronc saddle while it was on the ground. He'd adjusted the stirrup leathers, stretching his legs forward with his feet in the stirrups as he turned his toes out to get the right feel, making sure his butt was tight up against the cantle at the back of his saddle. But the butterflies in his gut were giving him some grief, he later recounted.

Val carefully placed the saddle on his bronc, high up on its withers. He checked his front cinch to make sure it was straight up and down. Then he checked the back cinch, making sure it was behind the last rib of his horse, and then he put his buck rein through the halter, making sure the end of the loop was pointing upward so he wouldn't spur over his rein.

To make sure his riding hand was in exactly the right place, he pulled the rein tight against the base of the horse's mane, then flipped it over the horse's head to its eye on the other side. He pulled his rein over the swells of his saddle plus a hand and two fingers. Finding both measurements the same, he marked the spot with a couple of mane hairs. His prep work finished, he focused on calming the butterflies.

Taking a good, deep seat in the saddle once again, he lifted on his buck rein and gave the nod. The gate opened, and his bronc reared up and out into the air. When the horse's feet came down, so did its head, taking all the slack out of Val's buck rein. Suddenly Val's elbow dropped. Instead of lifting, he pulled on his buck rein. In a rapid flash, the rein pulled him up and out of his saddle, which gave him the sensation of flying.

Val said, "That first jump out of the chute felt much different in a bronc saddle than holding on to the handle of a bareback rigging. It was completely different than anything I had ever experienced. There was no handle to hold on to. It was all balance and timing. That buck rein didn't seem to help much either. All that horse wanted to do was try to pull me over his front end. I certainly didn't want that to happen. Losing my timing right out of the chute, I landed in the dirt after a couple of good jumps."

Robert was the next SideKick to ride a saddle bronc at Richfield. He marked his horse out as they left the chute. His legs moved in rhythm with his bronc, and he was on his way to making a qualified ride, maybe even placing. As his horse would rear up, Robert's feet would go back toward the cantle of his saddle. As his horse's front feet hit the ground, Robert's feet were in home position, extended forward in the stirrup with his toes pointing outward. He appeared to have things under control until his spur snagged the rear cinch of his bronc saddle. Suddenly daylight was between him and his saddle and he made an early exit.

Val climbed on his first bull at this rodeo. He said, "I felt more fear riding a bull than riding that bronc. A horse can hurt you, but a bull can do you in. I knew that if I screwed up on this ride, things could turn ugly. Leaving the chute, I felt more power from this bull than my bronc horse. I think that pure adrenalin rush I experienced was tied more to what that bull could do to me. That rush stayed with me for three or four jumps before I landed in the dirt. Then I thought, *Wow, that was fun.* It was in Richfield that Val made history, becoming the first SideKick to participate in all three rough-stock events in a single high school rodeo.

Shorty rode a bull named 22 Stub. About four seconds into his ride, he felt his bull rope slipping. Just as he was thinking the rope didn't feel right, it broke and he landed on his feet, still holding on to it.

One of the bull riders from another school had landed hard and appeared to be injured. Slash C's stock contractor and the guy in charge of the rodeo, Bill Crittenden (see appendix), was anxious for the rodeo to keep moving and jokingly said, "Just throw the cowboy over the fence and let's go on with this rodeo." Unfortunately, Clint heard the remark just before it was his turn to ride. When the bull charged out of the chute, Clint was thrown off and got stepped on. Laying in the dirt and hurting, Clint looked up at Bill and, with a slight smile on his face, said, "Bill, don't throw me over the fence; I will get up." Laughter rippled through the arena as Clint got up on his feet with some help.

* * *

In Ogden at the old indoor Golden Spike arena, Richard Rigby again tried his bull-riding skills on White Dove, owned by Cross Triangle Rodeo Company. This big gray Brahma hurt your groin muscles just looking at him.

Coming out of the chute, White Dove kicked high, then came down hard. The bull turned into Richard's hand and then went the other way. Richard hung on with every ounce of strength he could muster through some intense moments. When his right hand began to weaken, he quickly took another seat—this time in the dirt.

Richard felt it was one of his better bull rides as he'd managed to stay on the bull the longest of any at that point in his bull-riding career.

Darryl Peel became interested in riding rough stock while riding in the kids' rodeo during Hub City's Fourth of July celebration. He'd won at several of the kids' events, so he decided to keep at it when high school rodeo became available.

Darryl drew Cross Western, a big gray Brahma with its horns pointing upward, owned by the Cross Triangle Rodeo Company. It was Darryl's first bull ride—and his last. Before he could climb down on the bull in the chute, he had to wait for the bull rider who'd ridden before him to be hauled out of the arena on a stretcher. "That kind of messed up my concentration," Darryl said. "When I finally nodded for the gate to open, my bull made a quick side flip with his hind end and came out of the chute making a series of crazy moves." Darryl lost both his grip and his boot at about the same time. As he landed, the bull ran one way and Darryl the other.

Darryl rode a bareback bronc named Instant Trouble at that same rodeo. He liked riding bareback broncs better than bulls because he had grown up riding horses on a farm, and horses were his comfort zone. Darryl's bronc came out of the chute and gave him a good ride—for about six seconds. But what happened at the rodeo didn't compare to the thrills he and some of the boys experienced on their way home, somewhere between Springville and Spanish Fork.

According to Darryl, he was driving Casey's 1972 Ford pickup when things suddenly didn't feel right. He later said, "When we saw one of our tires rolling down the highway ahead of us, I realized what had happened. I managed to maintain control as I pulled Casey's truck over to the side of the highway. Someone had picked up our tire on the highway and brought it back to us. We were able to get some lug nuts at the hardware store, put the tire back on, and headed on home."

* * *

We saw some great things and learned some important lessons that second year of high school rodeo. It's difficult to measure exactly how much the kids had grown in self-esteem and confidence, but they had. And what's to boot is that there was a measurable improvement in their academic performance. Some were even graduating—something that wouldn't have happened without their participation in rodeo. If they'd seen such an improvement in high school, I wondered what their rodeo experiences might do for them in the arena of life.

CHAPTER ELEVEN

"El Toro"

A Lesson Learned: Self-Confidence Builds Success

E L Toro," a new, $2,500 mechanical bucking machine pur-chased by the school district, had been unloaded into the shop building, and we were anxious to try it out, but there was one major setback: We couldn't use the shop building. We could store it there, but we couldn't ride it. The basketball coach said it was too big to put in the gym. It was obvious we were in Hawks Club territory and that he was not going move over to make room for us. It was much like getting a battery-operated toy without batteries.

Our needs were pretty simple—an electrical outlet and shel-ter. Oh, and a little heat would be welcome during the winter. After several months, we received word that the district would provide the materials if the Rodeo Club members would build a structure to house El Toro, and so we started sizing up our re-sources. SideKick Danny Livingston could help; his father had taught him how to lay bricks. Mr. Thornton, our vice principal, was a carpenter and had built houses. Excitement mounted as we began to believe we could do it.

When the building materials arrived, the SideKicks—both girls and boys—went right to work. By March 24, 1977, the SideKicks had a new rodeo gym—a fully enclosed 400-square-foot cinderblock building with double doors facing south and windows facing east and north. Our rodeo gym stood proudly at the northeast corner of the high school next to the football field.

Unfortunately, not everyone was pleased with what the SideKicks had achieved in building their gym. Chief among our detractors was an English teacher who'd had a classroom with a view. Until we'd built our gym, she could see the football field from her desk. She wasn't happy. But the SideKicks were thrilled and profusely thanked all who had helped make their dream come true.

After we got El Toro set up in our new building, Shorty couldn't wait—he jumped on and gave the nod. He soon experienced what it felt like to hit the concrete floor and decided to wait until we attached a bull rope and put a good layer of sawdust down.

El Toro was designed to simulate both the actions of a bucking horse and a bull. It spun and bucked at varied speeds but could be kept under control at all times to prevent riders from being injured. Members could practice their riding techniques before climbing aboard a live, bucking animal. We used a bull rope to simulate riding a bull and bareback rigging to simulate riding a bareback bronc. Many of our students were able to master the beast, but several got tossed around by El Toro throughout the remainder of that school year—and even throughout the next school year and the one after that.

Rodeo Club members worked with El Toro every Wednesday evening to perfect their riding style, timing, and the other fine arts of riding a bucking animal. Before long we had girls and even adults trying El Toro. It was the closest some ever came to riding the real thing. El Toro even became a family affair as SideKicks brought their brothers, sisters, and sometimes parents to ride.

My wife even rode that machine, and later our children did too. After watching several people ride El Toro at full speed, Shannon—my then-seven-year-old daughter—was hesitant but climbed aboard anyway. Expecting the worst, she gave us the signal. We cranked it down so she could experience El Toro in slow motion. My three-year-old son was last to climb aboard; he demonstrated how to ride our mechanical bull with a bottle in your mouth.

I remember watching Ted Mollinet easily ride El Toro at full speed. I think someone could have thrown him a hot dog while he was riding. In fact, he probably could have garnished it with mustard and pickle relish and thrown it back. It wasn't long before Ted was riding bareback bronc horses under the SideKick banner.

SideKick Kevin Thompson loved to ride El Toro, demonstrating perfect form and technique. It looked like he and the machine were one. Horse trainer Dean Barney maintained that El Toro must have helped Kevin become a better rider. Long after Kevin graduated, I watched him stay in perfect control on a bucking buckskin mare, something I was sure El Toro had played a part in.

There was only one problem: El Toro didn't have a head, which meant we couldn't get the feel of lifting the buck rein on El Toro. To compensate, we tried having someone pull the rein from the front as a rider lifted on the buck rein; using that technique, a rider could get an idea of how things might feel as a horse's head went up and down in a bucking motion. Even then, as SideKicks transferred from El Toro to a real saddle bronc, the buck rein assumed a whole different feel—El Toro bucked and turned in place. Bucking horses did not.

TED MOLLINET "BUCKWHEAT" NORTH SANPETE H.S. RODEO MANTI 1977

After years of use, El Toro finally wore itself out. SideKicks, their family members, and their friends had had a lot of fun on El Toro. It had served its purpose in fostering friendships, building memories, and improving self-confidence.

Today, the old high school has been torn down, but the rodeo gym building still stands. As I pass that old cinderblock structure near where the old high school once stood, memories of El Toro suddenly come alive. More than three decades later, I can still hear the laughter and excitement. El Toro replaced negative labels with positive feelings among SideKicks and others as friendships were formed. The students had begun looking out for each other as they moved from El Toro to high school rodeo competition. With our new bronc saddle and El Toro, the SideKicks' adventures continued at a whole new level.

There were times when I felt my responsibility to be heavy, especially as I became more involved in my students' lives.

However, something inside kept telling me that what we were doing for those students was worth all the effort. I saw it elevate their character, self-worth, and desire to stay in school. It was about this time that I received the following letter from Lloyd Smith at Central Utah Educational Services, addressed to Superintendent Royal Allred, North Sanpete School District:

> *This is information that you may wish to share with the North Sanpete School Board. We have recently become aware of the outstanding program that has been made available with students at the North Sanpete High School. We are pleased to note the increased interest and involvement of students who might otherwise have been failures, disruptive influences or dropouts.*
>
> *It is our observation that establishing a rodeo club has provided a learning experience and a motivation for students to stay in school. We commend your foresight in recognizing the need for students to be involved in extracurricular activities.*
>
> *We are well aware that it is often through these extra activities that young people develop self-esteem, self-confidence, leadership, and acceptance of their peers. We commend you as a school board for your support of this rodeo club and for your contribution of El Toro. We were pleased to see the high school administration providing their support to this fine program. Back-up support from you, the administration of the district, and the high school personnel has resulted in a fine educational program. Perhaps it should be noted that*

*the rodeo program appears to upgrade this program in
the eyes of the entire student body. The Rodeo Club and
its activities, being opened to all students, could benefit
many students.*

Another letter I received helped me realize that the sacrifices
we had made were worth it. Shane Walters' younger brother,
Jody, not a SideKick, wrote, "I remember those 'whipper
snappers,' 'boot huggers,' and 'buckle bunnies' kicking around
that mechanical bull. It was a big deal back then to have El Toro
in that cinderblock building. Being at the controls was as fun as
riding the machine. Those were certainly good days for learning
about the bumps and bruises that were to come later in life."

Jody knew all about the hard knocks and bruises of life—
he'd gone to prison for an alcohol-related incident. Though
not a former SideKick, he loved horses, and he was one of a
select group of inmates chosen to take care of the prison's
fifteen hundred horses. Jody wasn't afraid to get on the backs
of those rank critters. In his letter, which I received while he
was in prison, he wrote, "Those desert horses are mean. They
eat rocks and cactus. When they get you out of the saddle, they
'aim' with those unshod hooves as you are fallin'. It looks like
you are huntin' worms when you hit the dirt."

Some of our SideKicks certainly appeared to be looking for
worms out in the dirt from time to time. But as they gained
experience in riding skills, these students began shifting their
rodeo adventures into overdrive.

CHAPTER TWELVE

Sponsoring Our First High School Rodeo

A Lesson Learned: Extracurricular Activities Promote Camaraderie

Rusty Bench had been elected rodeo club president, with John Larsen as vice president, Sharie Stevens as secretary, Ann Mickkelsen as treasurer, and Kelly Simons as club historian when we got the opportunity to host our first qualified high school rodeo. Excitement throughout the club rose as we all began making preparations.

We signed a contract with Slash C Rodeo Company out of Francis, Utah. They agreed to provide the livestock, rodeo clowns, judges, and pickup men for a total of $1,350. The Side-Kicks began advertising early on, hoping to gain school and community support. We hoped to have at least half the number of spectators that normally came to the high school's football and basketball games.

Our female members took care of the many entries that came in. The entry fees back then were six dollars if a contestant did not need the stock contractor to provide an animal and ten dollars if an animal needed to be furnished.

With twelve full events, the SideKicks rodeo was fully approved by the Utah State High School Rodeo Association, and it generated a great deal of interest throughout the state's high school rodeo clubs. Sponsors donated $1,000 for the awards that would be presented to the winners in each event.

The club members, now numbering thirty, wanted to have their first high school rodeo in Mount Pleasant, but that wasn't possible; the old Mount Pleasant arena was so old that it was unsafe. We had to find an adequate and safe arena for the event, and the Sanpete County fairgrounds in Manti was our best option. The county gave us permission to use their facilities, and we reserved the arena for the last weekend in May.

"Looking back, I think of all the work that went into getting things ready for this event," Ann Mikkelsen reflected. "I remember typing up the rodeo program—if only we could have had a word processor!" Ann was helped by Linda Larsen, a teacher's assistant who was truly loved by SideKicks.

We were fortunate to have one of today's top rodeo photographers recording the event. Jim Fain provided the SideKicks with some mighty super shots, some of which are featured in this book. His wife, the former Karen Johnson of Fountain Green, was a graduate of North Sanpete High School. We were honored that they were a working part of North Sanpete High School rodeo history.

Jim grew up in Phoenix, Arizona. He met Karen while working at the North Rim of the Grand Canyon during the summer of '61. They were married in '64. Jim graduated from Utah State University with bachelor's and master's degrees in photography. Today, he claims over fifty years of rodeo photography at high school rodeo finals, college rodeo finals, and pro-rodeo national finals.

Of his experiences photographing these events, Jim says, "The older I get, the more I value those photos that were taken of me doing my rodeo rides. I don't have many. However, when I look at them, I can still smell the rosin and the sweat of the horses. I can even feel the pain of a broken leg." Memories from decades ago are now brought back to life for the SideKicks through the lens of Jim's camera.

Leesa, another one of our SideKicks, was especially excited about our upcoming rodeo because it would give her and the other members a chance to shine. As the first home rodeo for the SideKicks, it gave North Sanpete the chance to make history once again. Leesa said, "Everyone in the club was going to participate. Some other girls and I were asked to carry the flag in the grand entry. Every night for two weeks, I went home and rode my horse to get him ready. Then, two days before the rodeo, my sister and I got in a fight. We started to yell at each other, and as she started to walk away, I kicked her. My foot got as big as a watermelon. I couldn't even walk on it, let alone ride, so I ended up sitting on the bench at our rodeo."

We were expecting two hundred entries but ended up with 227 from rodeo clubs throughout the state. Sadly, our spectator attendance was less than expected for both nights, but that didn't dampen our spirits. The stock was rank and bucked hard. The contestants performed well, and the action was fast-paced. I was amazed at the fine horsemanship and true sportsmanship those high school youth displayed. Our expenses were paid entirely by money raised by the club members, contestant entry fees, gate receipts, and food sales. The club even ended up with a few hundred dollars in profit after all the bills were paid.

Some great things came out that rodeo. Ted Mollinet drew a bareback bronc named Buckwheat, a Slash C horse. As he gave the nod, the gate flew open, and his bronc entered the arena like a torpedo. Though he didn't know quite what to expect, Ted got two or three good jumps out of that ride before he took a dive into the dirt.

Shorty took his first ride on a bareback bronc at this rodeo. When he climbed aboard Silver Dollar and nodded for the gate to open, his horse came out cranking hard. Shorty rode Silver Dollar until the whistle blew; making a qualified ride, he ended up in fourth. "That bronc ride was awesome," Shorty later said, "but I felt more comfortable on a bull. I had to work harder to stay on that bareback than on any bull I had ever ridden."

Shorty had been herding sheep between Indianola and Fountain Green at the time and had to walk nine and a half miles to where he could catch a ride to our rodeo in Manti. His father had gotten Shorty a summer job in the hope of keeping him away from the girls, and Shorty regularly had to walk or hitchhike to town. It was a real accomplishment for him to place at our first rodeo in his first bareback bronc-riding experience, especially after the long road he'd taken to get there.

The magic of Shorty's victory wasn't lost on his teammates. Tim said, "I watched as Shorty came out of that chute on Silver Dollar. That horse really cut loose. I stood amazed as I watched him ride that bronc for the full eight seconds. What a ride, especially considering it was his first time on a bareback bronc."

Others agreed, as did I. Shorty demonstrated that toughness is in the mind. Small in stature, he knew how to use his body to his advantage whether on a bronc or bull. Shorty also drew a bull by the name of Diamond Back, a crossbred Hereford with horns that narrowed to a point. Though he was fun to ride, Diamond Back just didn't give Shorty the points he needed to place in bull riding. Shorty managed to stay in control from the get-go, then jumped off after he heard the buzzer sound.

Jimmy CHRISTENSEN   NORTH SANPETE H.S. RODEO - MANTI 1977

He said, "The harder I kicked, the faster he ran. It was not very hard for me to stay on that bull."

Jimmy Christensen rode a bareback bronc named Lefty. He showed pure grit as he stayed aboard even after the whistle blew. He ended up with fifth-place honors. SideKick Garth Edmunds also made a good first attempt on a bareback bronc named Half Pint. Coming out of the chute, Garth appeared to be in control until he got stretched out from his rigging. Not able to get his timing synced with his bronc, his feet caused him to lose his seat, and off he flew. In bull riding, Tim placed second among the thirty-one riders in that event. It was the second time that season Tim had taken second place, and he was well on his way to a chance for a state championship in bull riding.

When it was all over, the All-Around Cowgirl Saddle Award went to Ogden, the All-Around Cowboy Award to Richfield.

Our rodeo queen was also from Ogden. Ann was chosen as one of the queen's attendants by judges selected from the State High School Rodeo Association. Ann said, "This high school rodeo turned out to be one of the best high school rodeos in the state. Several of us qualified for state during 1977. We were really an up-and-coming club. That was a great time in our lives, and I will always treasure those memories." Our rodeo became one of the highlights of the SideKicks' high school rodeo experiences. It allowed them to shine in every way in front of their peers, neighbors, and friends. As with the others we attended, our rodeo enhanced SideKick character development, self-esteem, and self-confidence.

Thanks to the efforts and support of many, our first rodeo went off without a hitch. Afterward, the SideKicks had a new spring in their step. More laughter was heard in their inner circle, and any vestiges of depression and lack of focus were replaced with such things as self-worth and being a part of something important.

CHAPTER THIRTEEN

Mickey Young Seminar

A Lesson Learned: A Good Role Model Creates Positive Effects

PROFESSIONAL rodeo cowboy and national finalist Mickey Young had a positive impact on the SideKicks during his visit to North Sanpete. Not only did he teach principles about correctly riding bareback bronc horses, but he also became a valued mentor. Mickey came to us from over the mountain, where he then lived in Wellington, Utah. He was one of three Utah cowboys to have ever qualified for the National Finals Rodeo.

Our Mickey Young bareback bronc riding seminar was held in the old Mount Pleasant arena and at the high school in March 1978, just a few months after Mickey had competed as a national finalist in bareback bronc riding a second time at the National Finals Rodeo in Oklahoma City. The seminar featured demonstrations, lectures, films, a dinner program, and bareback bronc riding.

Shorty showed up at the seminar on crutches, so Bobby Hardman—a student with some size and strength—became his packhorse. He even carried Shorty up the steps of the high school—a "mere" three stories.

Upon Mickey's arrival at North Sanpete, he was sitting at tenth in the national standings as a bareback bronc rider. Mickey had also won the Bareback Bronc Riding Championship for the

Wilderness Circuit—comprised of Utah, Idaho, and Nevada—that year. His other honors included winnings at some of the top rodeos in the United States and Canada, including the Calgary Stampede and the Cow Palace Rodeo. We were thrilled to have Mickey come to our high school. The banquet and program were well attended by club members, seminar students, their parents, school and district administrators, and school board members and their wives; more than one hundred people showed up. Mickey shared how he'd started in rodeo and talked about his hard times and his good times.

Rusty, past president of the SideKicks, entertained those attending the banquet with a couple of songs. Rusty had the looks of a handsome, rugged cowboy, and the country sound he produced could melt any cowgirl's heart. He left us all wanting to hear more. Bill Lewis, the National High School Rodeo director from Spanish Fork, spoke on the availability of rodeo scholarships, educational loans, and career opportunities through the National Rodeo Association. Jay Quarnberg, our North Sanpete High School rodeo announcer from the Tooele area, told of his experiences with high school rodeos since 1958. He shared his observations of high school rodeo and its positive effects on youth.

During the day, bronc-riding action took place under the watchful eye of Mickey out at the old Mount Pleasant arena. Slash C Rodeo Company had brought a load of bucking horses the day before, and cowboys from throughout the state took rides on those broncs, learning from their mistakes with Mickey's tutoring.

The SideKicks enrolled in the seminar included Ted Mollinet, Casey Larsen, Lauren Larsen, Blake Nielsen, Jon Larsen,

Arnold Moosman, Jimmy Christensen, Garth Edmunds, Brett Hope, Clint Lynch, Wade Christensen, Kelly Poulsen, Kevin Thompson, and Shane Walters. As they gathered in front of the old wooden bucking chutes for a group picture, one could not help but notice how old the facility was—but it was the best we had, so we made it work.

When I noticed Clint Lynch's name on the list of attendees, I asked his brother Jerry if Clint had ever ridden a bronc in a rodeo. "Clint got on two bareback broncs," Jerry told me. "They both threw him higher than a kite. When the second one threw him off, I heard a laugh as he said, 'This is crazy! I am going back to riding bulls.'"

Mickey showed his students how to keep their toes pointed outward during a bronc ride; he even advised them to practice walking with their toes that way. He told them that while he and the others cowboys had been in Houston before their rodeo, they'd practiced this as they'd walked down the street. "People there probably thought we were a little nutty," Mickey said with a laugh.

Once, while we were watching a rodeo from the bleachers, we noticed a bronc rider heading straight toward us with his toes pointing straight out. The person sitting next to me said, "Look, that cowboy has his boots on the wrong feet." Taking another look, I realized it was true. We had a good laugh as I remembered Mickey telling his students to get those toes out—but I'm sure he didn't intend that they put their boots on the wrong feet.

Mickey even took advantage of El Toro to teach technique. He showed the students how to get their feet to home position, telling them to drag them back as far as possible toward their rigging, then charge them again forward to home position before the horse's front feet hit the ground again. All the students tried it on El Toro, then experienced a whole new challenge on a real animal out in the arena.

On his way out, Mickey tacked a note to our bulletin board that read, "SideKicks, positive attitudes are the key to success. Give 101% all the time." Mickey also gave the SideKicks a large print of him riding a bronc. We decoupaged the picture and placed it on our classroom's "Wall of Rodeo Fame." At the bottom of the print were the words, *Positive Attitudes Are the Key to Success.* A positive mentor, Mickey helped us understand what went into the making of a champion. He went the extra mile in showing the kids that he cared about them individually.

"While Mickey was in town, he dropped by our house and spent some time with us," Jerry said. "He saw we were poor. My mother had paid for Val to take his seminar, but she couldn't afford to pay for all of us. But Mickey never excluded any of us from his seminar. We let him use our practice horses, and he gave us pointers. Mickey took the time to help all of us."

Blake Nielson said he owed a lot of his bronc riding success to Mickey Young. "He was really good to me," he said. "When I attended his bronc riding school in Price, he helped me out a lot there also. He even remembered me from the SideKicks seminar in Mount Pleasant. Jon Larsen and I rode twenty-two head of bucking horses in those three days at Mickey's school in Price. It was difficult for us to find practice stock, but we thought this was our opportunity, so we put it to our advantage."

Mickey and his new bride, Lori, stayed at our house. We let them sleep in our bed, and we went into another room. After that, my wife began telling family members, "We do not give up our bed to relatives—only to rodeo people."

While writing this memoir, I watched on television as Josi, Mickey and Lori's son, rode bareback broncs as the season's leader in the Professional Rough Stock Association. As I watched Josi make a good bareback ride, I realized how much time had slipped away since Mickey's seminar at our school. Time really does fly.

Along with our bronc saddle, El Toro, and the rodeo building, Mickey Young's visit proved to be another powerful incentive for the SideKicks to take things that much further.

CHAPTER FOURTEEN

At State

A Lesson Learned: Having Fun Is Part of the Contest

LESS THAN A MONTH after we sponsored that first rodeo, the SideKicks found themselves participating at the State Finals in Heber. It was evident the stock contractors hadn't held back on the kinds of livestock they'd brought to the finals. The bucking stock was rank. High school rodeo cowboys and cowgirls had a challenge ahead of them as the competition was among the best in the state.

The years seem to have flown by as I recall that event. There were some of the most memorable rides in SideKicks history. Tim drew a Kirby bull with no name other than #125. Kirby bulls were owned by "Swany" Kirby, owner of Bar T Rodeo Company (see appendix). Bar T has produced PRCA-sanctioned rodeos in our area for years. At that time, the company was known for its great bucking bulls, several of which had performed at the National Finals Rodeo in Oklahoma City.

In addition to the boys who qualified for state, we had three girls qualify—Ann Mikkelsen, Crystal Watson, and Heidi McKay. Ann made us proud as the first girl from North Sanpete High School to compete in the queen contest. She had also qualified to compete in barrel racing.

Waiting for her turn for the cloverleaf pattern, Ann watched competitive times being posted in her category. She felt the pressure, and the adrenalin started to flow as she heard her name called. She entered the arena as if she were spurring a racehorse down the track at full speed. She grabbed the saddle horn with one hand as her horse approached the first barrel. But as she was getting ready to make that first turn, her horse blew a fuse—he decided he was *not* going to make that first turn, though he'd done it on all his practice runs. He became uncooperative and broke the pattern, which disqualified Ann. Had that not happened, Ann could have won top honors at State Finals. One can only imagine her disappointment. I'm sure a love-hate relationship existed between Ann and her horse as they traveled back home together.

Heidi was the next SideKick to compete. The competition in the queen contest was stiff; the outfits the girls wore were absolutely stunning, and to be in the top ten was an honor. Of the twenty-four contestants, Heidi was named third runner-up to Miss Utah High School Rodeo. Heidi also qualified in the goat-tying contest. She and her horse came into that arena at twenty miles per hour. Approaching the goat, which was staked to a ten-foot rope, she slowed and got out of her saddle, riding in the stirrup for a moment. Stepping onto the ground at a run, she quickly caught the goat, lifted him off the ground, set him down, gathered up his feet, and made the tie with a quick wrap and a half hitch. Holding her breath and hoping her goat remained tied, she stepped away from it and waited for seven long seconds. While Heidi's time seemed fast, it was not fast enough for her to place in the top four. She had to be in the eight-second range. Imagine her frustration when she learned she had missed placing by less than a second.

In barrel racing, Crystal came into her first barrel at full speed, pulling her horse a little to the outside as it entered the pocket.

Making a clean turn around that first barrel, just barely touching it, she headed to the second. It was a little wide but clean, and she had only one barrel left in her cloverleaf pattern. As she arrived at the third barrel, her horse made the turn a little wide, costing Crystal valuable time on the clock, but she headed home at full speed and ended up twelfth among fifty contestants.

Crystal also competed in pole bending, where winners and losers are often separated by one-tenth, sometimes even one-hundredth, of a second. Crystal's horse weaved down through each pole and back again. She tapped a couple of poles on the last weave but thankfully did not knock any over, which would have cost her a five-second penalty per pole. After going around the end pole, she hustled across the finish line. Crystal made a good, clean run but did not place in the top four. A rider had to be in the nineteen-second range to place, and Crystal was in the twenties.

I was proud of both our girls and boys as they rose to the occasion at state. Coming out of the chute, Tim was in control as he managed to use his free arm to his advantage. He didn't want to get wild with that free arm because it could drop him "down into the well"—the inside spin of the bull. It was obvious Tim had a lot of bull under him. This big gray bull, with its huge hump and wicked set of horns, was indeed a handful. It kicked high and fierce, moving first to the right and then to the left. Tim continued to bear down hard, but a sudden move to the right with a high sideway kick ripped him out of his bull rope. Tim's ride ended too short for a score—but the seconds he stayed on that bull seemed to last an eternity.

As I relived that experience in my mind, I recalled Tim sharing his first bull-riding experience with me. "I was scared as Uncle Rex and Shorty cinched me up," Tim said. "Everyone began telling me what to do, and I simply signaled them to open the gate. When the bull entered the arena, I was doing okay until I got strung out on my bull rope. When that happened, the bull whipped me down real quick. Even though I went off before eight seconds, I felt good—I had met a challenge." Tim had met yet another challenge at state, and he had done it honorably.

When it came time for Robert Draper to climb aboard his bronc, he took ahold of his buck rein exactly where he'd placed a couple of horsehairs through his braided rope. He ran the buck rein in between his ring finger and his little finger and tightly closed his fist. As he lifted on the rein, he leaned back and nodded for the gate.

His bronc burst out of the chute, high in the air. Robert hung those spurs over the point, making the mark-out rule, and then his feet went forward and back to the cantle of his saddle. He continued to stay in time, looking as though he were in control, just what the judges liked to see. And he remained glued to that horse until the pick-up man rescued him. Robert's saddle bronc ride put him in first place in the second section of the first go-round. With that win, it appeared Robert was in the right place at the right time—and on his way to becoming a state champion.

During the next go-round, Robert's saddle bronc came out of the chute fast and wild. Robert stuck his spurs into his bronc's shoulder. After a good spur out, he began raking his bronc, staying in time with the kick and drop of the animal. With his toes turned out, his thighs were glued tightly beneath the swells of his saddle. With that fantastic ride, Robert became the SideKicks' first state champion, bringing fourth-place honors back to North Sanpete High School. What a great moment for him as he made history during his last year in high school.

Val, the first to qualify for state in bareback bronc riding, drew a Kerby bronc named Roan Light. Val was going from competing in regular high school rodeos to competing with an elite group of high school cowboys who were at the top of their game on some of the better bucking stock in the state. As soon as the gate opened, Roan Light jumped in the air. Val put forth a valiant effort to bring his feet to home place before his bronc's front feet connected with the ground. He wanted to have both of his boot heels over the point of the shoulder on that first jump out of the chute.

After that big buck out, Roan Light remained strong and powerful throughout his journey around the arena. Val remained aggressive, scratching his bronc's neck on each jump as he rode his bronc until the horn sounded. It made a good ride for Val—at least I *thought* so until I heard the announcer say, "No score!" Val had missed his bronc out at the chute, giving him a score of zero for what had been a mighty effort. He was not happy after having made a such good bronc ride at state, and you could see his disappointment as he made the long walk back to the bucking chutes.

At first, the SideKicks struggled with the mark-out rule, where the rider's spurs had to touch the animal above the point of the shoulder on the first jump out of the shoot. Eventually, they began to realize its benefit. The rule helped them to stay ahead in their timing and to get into the rhythm of their bronc at the beginning of their ride. Once they figured that out, more SideKicks began staying on their broncs and getting off with the help of the pick-up man.

On the next bronc in his second go-around, Val looked good. His bronc remained strong and bucked aggressively. Yet even with all that horsepower in Val's hand, he managed to ride to the big eight, earning him sixty-eight points. His extra effort to make the mark-out rule paid off, giving Val a good score for high school competition.

After the state finals, Val began entering multiple events—bull riding, bareback bronc riding, saddle bronc riding, and team roping—becoming the first SideKick to compete in four events. I remember Val as being extremely levelheaded; not much seemed to rattle his cage.

The other SideKick to qualify for state in 1977 was Rusty Bench. He rode a Kerby horse named Hoot Owl who came out of the chute mighty fast. Rusty continued to give that ride his best effort until the sound of the whistle only to discover he had missed his horse out at the chute. However, he remains the first SideKick to qualify in the saddle bronc competition at state.

On his second go, Rusty drew a big bay by the name of Mouse, a Kerby horse that had been to the National Finals. That bronc jostled Rusty in a right-left shift, then took him into a spin, leaving him hanging on to his buck rein off center. But with pure cowboy grit, Rusty continued to hold on to his buck rein and stayed in contact with his bronc saddle.

Going into a spin can really mess up a cowboy's timing, and Rusty found it a challenge to get his inside foot in time with his bronc. Mouse was not an easy ride, but Rusty managed to keep his seat almost until the buzzer sounded.

After the State High School Rodeo Finals, Robert gained the spotlight in the town's newspaper, *The Pyramid*. The paper featured him as having earned a spot at the National Rodeo Championship Finals in Helena, Montana, coming up in August. Robert was the fourth-ranked saddle-bronc rider in the

State High School Rodeo Association. When the editor asked him about his experience at state, Robert responded by saying, "There was a lot of pressure competing for that number-one slot. But each contestant was willing to offer a helping hand as needed, even though the pressure and spirit of competition was high. Contestants remained concerned for the other guy."

Robert received a letter from the National High School Rodeo Association congratulating him on qualifying for the National Finals. We were proud of this letter, as it was a first for a SideKick member. Mr. Thornton, our vice principal, told me that the school district continued to lend us their support and had accepted my request for them to cover our expenses to Helena. Their generosity would enable Robert to participate at the National High School Finals, and it appeared everything was a go. The door was open for Robert to earn a National High School Saddle Bronc Championship.

Then the bad news arrived.

Robert had gotten himself into some trouble, and our trip to Montana had to be canceled.

I have often wondered why Robert allowed an opportunity such as this to go down the tubes, though I've never discussed that situation with him. I'm certain it was not out of fear; Robert was fearless about riding a bucking horse. He seemed to be in his element in a saddle on such a wild ride. The whole time a bronc was trying to put him on the arena floor, he remained loose and in time with the moves of his horse. So while Robert never made it to National Finals, I knew he'd loved his time in the saddle, and I hoped it would help him with whatever his future held.

* * *

It wasn't typical for our kids to get into trouble. While they definitely had fun participating in rodeo, they took being part of the club seriously. They were a respectful, hardworking bunch, and so it came as a surprise when, not long after state, the following letter arrived in the mail:

Dear Advisors:

It has been brought to our attention by the owners of the Ken Loma Motel that several rooms received $120 in damages consisting of broken chairs and broken flower pots; one room had watermelon on the ceiling and walls, which took several hours to clean up; and there were other things of this type. These damages were done by high school members during the State Finals.

There were four clubs involved in the damages. We feel that each club should pay its part of the damages done. The whole club will be on probation and will not be able to participate in rodeo until it is taken care of.

Those clubs involved were: Tooele, room 4;Huntington, room 5; Bear River, room 6; and North Sanpete, room 7. Advisors, this is serious and we will appreciate your help with this problem. We would hate to see a whole club be unable to rodeo because of a few members. Thank You,

Reed Stephens, President

The motel room was listed in Val's name, but I didn't tell him about the letter at the time. I had full confidence that my SideKicks had behaved themselves properly. They were not about to do anything that might jeopardize the school board's support; unlike other clubs, the SideKicks were direct representatives of their high school. They did not take that privilege for granted, and they served their school with pride and honor. Not for one minute had any of them ever caused me or the school concern. I paid the thirty-dollar fine and told no one— at least not then.

Many years later when I mentioned the incident and letter to Val, he didn't remember the watermelon, but he did remember Rusty breaking the flowerpot—Rusty had actually fallen into it. During those times, our boys were all so poor that we had to put five or six of them in a room. As a result, it was often a little crowded, and the damaged flowerpot had been an accident.

* * *

State was a great boon to SideKicks members. The district continued its support, and the kids were featured in the local and school newspapers most every week throughout their rodeo seasons. Headlines ranged from "SideKicks Hitting the Dirt" to "SideKicks Winning Top Honors" (see appendix).

Sometimes the headlines were not so good, however. One I will never forget read, "Bull Rider Hurt in Ogden." Tim, Shane, and Shorty had entered the Teenage Championship Rodeo at the old Golden Spike Coliseum in Ogden. Friday night, Shorty was thrown off the left side of the bull and had fallen beneath the animal. Shorty heard his leg pop as the bull stomped on it, jumped sideways, and fell down. Shorty jumped up to run from the bull, but he fell down and had to crawl, having sustained a compound fracture.

Tim said, "Shorty was an amazing rider. He made it all look so easy. He had the potential to excel as a rodeo rough-stock rider. But in Ogden he got a bad deal." Tim had to drive Shorty's car home while Shorty spent the night at the McKay-Dee Hospital. He was released with his leg in a cast, which had to be removed a few days later when his leg started to swell.

Once again I had to ask myself if this high school rodeo program was really worth the risk involved; I felt horrible, but I knew that the experiences at state had had a positive effect on those kids and would give them memories to last a lifetime.

Who would have ever guessed these students would be competing at state when the North Sanpete High School rodeo club began? Who would have guessed Robert would win fourth at state and be given an invitation to compete at the national level? In my mind, those students had hit a home run by just getting up to the plate.

CHAPTER FIFTEEN

SideKicks Shine

A Lesson Learned: Things Are Hard Before They Become Easy

MANY FELT Clint Lynch was a champion bull rider in the making. But that's not what was on Clint's mind—he enjoyed the challenge but didn't want to take it to a higher level. Val summed up the thoughts of many when he said, "Clint was the most talented rider of us boys. When he sat down on an animal, he usually scored high."

Clint rode a bull like poetry in motion, and watching him ride was pure entertainment. He always seemed to be a step ahead of the animal when he rode, actually moving with the bull, staying somewhat loose, keeping his chin down, and staying in tune. Prior to the Emery rodeo, he had won the bull-riding competition at the Juab High School Rodeo in Nephi.

At the Emery High School Rodeo, Clint had a great ride on a bull named Black Berry. As Clint settled himself down on the animal and nodded for the gate, Black Berry made one big jump out of that chute and then spun away from Clint's hand, but Clint continued to make the correct moves, keeping in rhythm with his bull. That, and keeping his elbow down as that bull continued to spin away from his hand was what gave Clint another qualified ride. We watched as he grabbed the tail of his bull rope, gave it a tug, and jumped back behind his bull, making a safe getaway.

Clint's brother Wade drew Pepper, a good Slash C bronc horse. As he climbed down onto his saddle, he placed his feet in a "ready spur out" position. Imagine a force trying to pull you off as you struggle to hang on and strive to maintain control at the same time. That's exactly what Wade experienced on this ride. Riding a bronc to the whistle in spite of the forces working against you is no easy task for any high school student, but Wade did it. That became his first qualified ride after eight or ten disappointing attempts at other rodeos. After that ride, he won first place in Bryce Canyon.

It took time and dedication to become really good. Brent Lusk, a local bronc rider, said, "I had to make several bronc rides before I really got to where I could pick up my timing on a consistent basis." When I asked why he kept wanting to get on bronc horses, he said, "I just wanted to get better at it."

Also at the Emery rodeo, Ted made a good attempt on Fox, a Nelsen and Allred bronc. It was a jump and rapid run out into the arena, and Ted stayed aggressive as he did his best to get in time with his bronc. But Ted got behind a bit, and the bronc ended up with the advantage. Ted went up, and gravity bought him back down for a crash landing. Picking himself up, however, he walked back to the bucking chutes with a smile on his face.

* * *

Jimmy entered the Cow Country High School Rodeo in Manila. After more than a five-hour drive, Jimmy went right to the bulletin board and saw that only one bronc rider had qualified, and that had been on the previous day. Jimmy watched each bronc rider get thrown before the whistle as he continued to mentally prepare himself for his ride.

CASEY LARSEN "CORD" NORTH SANPETE H.S. RODEO MANTI 1977

JON LARSEN #21 (BAR 1) UHSRA FINALS HEBER CITY 1977

ROB DRAPER "SHIFTER" (EARL) UHSRA FINALS HEBER CITY 1977

Jimmy was the last bronc rider to compete, with still only one rider having earned a score. All he had to do was make a qualified ride and he would take first or second place, qualifying for state. It would be no easy task, though—those broncs were mighty rank.

All pumped up for his ride, Jimmy placed his hand in the handle of his rigging. Scooting up close, he reminded himself that there had never been a bronc that couldn't be ridden, followed in rapid-fire succession by the thought that there had never been a cowboy that couldn't be thrown. But he began seeing himself as the cowboy who couldn't be thrown as he nodded for the gate to open.

Experiencing one wild ride, Jimmy found himself still kicking and sitting on his bronc when the whistle blew. Had he made the mark-out rule? He heard a score from the announcer and knew right away that his score would put him in second. Years later he reflected that the Kirby bronc he rode in Manila was as hard to cover as any bronc he had ever ridden.

The other SideKicks placing at high school rodeos that weekend were Casey and Lauren. Casey ended up with fourth-place honors in bareback bronc riding, and Lauren took fourth in bull riding. Rusty, who rode in St. George, didn't have a great experience in the saddle-bronc ride. The rodeo was held in the Sun Bowl, and he drew a Bundy Rodeo Company horse. When that bronc bucked Rusty off, he found out exactly how hard the grass was and walked away with a broken wrist.

* * *

Jon and Blake shared first-place honors at the Juab High School Rodeo that year. Jon qualified at state in all three rough-stock events—bareback, saddle bronc, and bull riding—a first for the SideKicks. Blake qualified in bareback bronc and bull riding. Blake and Jon had come to us from rival South Sanpete High, where they'd competed against North Sanpete in football and wrestling. As they participated under our banner, they reached out to help the other club members even though they'd competed against each of them. As the two scratched the necks of bucking horses and tickled the sides of mean bulls, they remained as cool as a couple of cucumbers. They were up against some fierce competition, but they were winners and believed in themselves, and this worked to their advantage.

* * *

One can only imagine what it feels like to perform center stage in a rodeo arena, the adrenalin kicking in after a successful ride. The SideKicks shined not only on the outside but on the inside as well. Their countenances showed how much they relished the competition and how honored they felt to represent their school. Watching their demeanor change and seeing a new light in their eyes was rewarding.

As a result of their participation in high school rodeo, the SideKicks were better able to deal with the curve balls being thrown at them in life. They realized they could do hard things. As a result, new opportunities cropped up, one of which was the prospect of a new rodeo arena in Mount Pleasant. We were told Mount Pleasant city was applying for a grant—a working grant, which meant that the SideKicks would get to help build the new arena, which might be completed in time for our second North Sanpete High School rodeo.

We were excited for the possibility and became thoroughly involved.

CHAPTER SIXTEEN

A New Arena and a Walk Down Memory Lane

A Lesson Learned: Giving Is More Rewarding Than Receiving

THE "WORKING GRANT" meant that the SideKicks and other community members would need to do the labor and that the grant would pay for the materials. We were asked to draw up arena plans and submit them to James Thornton, the city council member in charge of the grant and our vice principal. The SideKicks immediately began making measurements. The old arena was a large one, measuring 185 feet by 350 feet. I was told these measurements had been taken from the Ute Stampede arena in Nephi, home of an annual PRCA Pro Rodeo. To stay within our budget of $32,500 and to allow for more parking spaces, we had to downsize the new arena to 130 by 250.

As the SideKicks and other members of the community began tearing down the arena, a flood of memories was unleashed. This arena had been built in the fifties by members of the local riding club after the original arena, which had been built in the thirties, was torn down. For a few years in between, there had been a makeshift arena. My father told me he remembered going to a rodeo in Mount Pleasant back in the midforties; they'd put up a "snow fence" and parked their cars around the fence for reinforcement.

With a twinkle in his eye and a smile on his face, Chelsey Christensen, longtime mayor of Mount Pleasant, said, "I rode my horse to that rodeo. On the way home we jumped the creek; I went one way and my horse went the other."

Having an interest in the community's rodeo history, hometown boy Charlie McKay, ten years my senior, suggested we talk to Francis Carlson, one of the oldest living residents in town.

During our visit, Francis told us that the first arena had been built in the early thirties and had stood in the middle of where State Street now is. They had torn it down to put the highway through the south end of town at the bend. Not long after our visit, Francis passed away at the age of ninety-five.

I envisioned that old arena with its perimeter fence, no bucking chutes, and perhaps only a corral or two. Side-delivery chutes didn't exist in the thirties. My father told me that in those days they'd snub the bronc horse up to a saddle horse. Once the bronc was blindfolded and saddled, the cowboy climbed aboard. In my mind's eye I could see those old-time cowboys climbing up on a bronc, getting set, then saying, "Jerk it." Suddenly, the blindfold would come off and the snub rope would be detached. A bronc ride would begin with the cowboy holding on with both hands, then using one hand to wave his hat to the crowd as his ride continued.

Until at least the mid-forties, those rides continued not just for eight seconds but until the horse quit bucking. There were no rules back then; in fact, the only "rule" was to just hang on. Names such as Artie Jones, Abe Burton, Tug Brewer, and Chris Larsen—the old-time rodeo cowboys—surfaced during my visit with Francis. Chris's name was familiar to me. Born in 1901, he was John, Casey, and Tim's grandfather. My father, born in 1913, had mentioned on a couple of occasions what a good saddle bronc rider Chris Larsen had been. It was these cowboys who'd most likely helped build the old arena back in the early thirties. Now, more than half a century later, Chris's grandsons were involved in the building of a new hometown rodeo arena.

Mont Larsen, Chris's son and an uncle to the Larsen SideKicks, said, "My dad loved working with horses. He rode broncs all over the western part of the United States." With a twinkle in his eye and a smile on his face, he added, "There was a time when Dad asked a local rancher for a job helping with his sheep. He was seventeen at the time. That local rancher was John H. Seeley, one of the largest ranchers in this area back then. Along with ranchers W. D. Candland and Justus O. Seeley, they would run sheep out in the west desert during winter one year and then on the east desert the following year. During the summers, they took the sheep to open range in the mountains and to their private land. Seeley had more than fifty employees working for him until the Taylor Grazing Act of 1934 changed the way federal lands were used for livestock production.

"Before Seeley agreed to hire my father, Dad had to ride an unbroken horse they were leading behind a camp wagon as they followed the sheep through town. My father put his saddle on that horse, pulled the cinch tight, and climbed aboard right there in the heart of downtown Mount Pleasant. The horse immediately ducked its head and started to buck. They smashed right into the big front window of F. C. Jensen's Consolidated Furniture store. The horse bucked around inside the store for a bit and finally came back out through the same window. My dad rode him until he quit bucking."

Having proved his mettle, that young cowboy followed the sheep out of town and headed for the west desert, a journey of more than a hundred miles. Today as I drive north down State to where Main intersects it, I sometimes find the stoplight turning red. It gives me a few minutes to look across to what is now Beck's Home Furnishings. The large plate-glass window remains as I relive the story of Chris Larsen and his horse. Can you imagine the look on Seeley's face that day?

* * *

The SideKicks remain proud to have been working part in the rebuilding of that arena in 1978. By way of their original petition for a high school rodeo, the new Mount Pleasant rodeo arena became a reality. It has since housed high school rodeos, 4-H activities, and the Hub City Days annual rodeo, in addition to many other horse-related activities through the years.

Sponsoring Our Second High School Rodeo

A Lesson Learned: Innovation Stimulates Motivation

J AMES THORNTON, who had been a great support to the Side-Kicks as vice principal, was now the principal of North Sanpete. We were so grateful for the support he'd given us in getting a new arena as he'd served on the city council. Dean Daniels was now the SideKicks club president, with Heidi McKay as secretary, Clint Lynch as historian, and Tracy Ivory as reporter. The club was now thirty-three members strong, twenty-two of whom were also members of the National High School Rodeo Association—which meant they were active rodeo contestants.

The biggest drawback for our members was getting parental permission or/and support. It was a big step for some parents to allow their sons or daughters to climb on a bronc or a mean bull for eight seconds. For others, coming up with the money and time to allow their child to participate was a steep mountain for them to climb.

* * *

As the time approached for our second North Sanpete High School Rodeo, the SideKicks hurried to get the new arena completed. The towns' excitement exploded when it became known that our high school rodeo was going to be held in the city's new arena. Local businesses continued to sponsor SideKicks by purchasing the awards for event winners. However, it remained to be seen how much interest the rodeo would get from the high school faculty and student body.

All rodeo events are enjoyable to watch, but bull riding seems to capture the most interest among spectators, probably because it is considered the most dangerous. When it came time to step up to the plate, the fearless members of our club were ready to ride Slash C's bulls. As always, we hoped there wouldn't be any injuries. To help ease concerns, Bill Crittenden had furnished some good bullfighters. One of these was Dean Stead from Ogden, a man with a reputation for saving cowboys. He was also a class act when it came to entertaining spectators, which was another reason we had requested him.

Weighing in at 167 pounds, Shane Walters, "Chief," rode a Slash C bull named Al Capone, a bull that weighed nearly a ton. As he left the chute, Al Capone fired out with both hind feet and went to the left, away from Chief's hand, and then back into it as they moved down the arena. But Chief managed to hang on, probably because he was afraid to get thrown; Al Capone had a reputation of trying to hurt cowboys when they were thrown. He had a set of horns that would have looked good on any wall. To sit on the back of that bull and look at those horns would have rattled anyone's nerves.

Chief rode his bull as though his hand was glued to his bull rope, and he ended up with second-place honors. Chief had started out riding bareback broncs, then saddle broncs, but after his ride that day he felt more natural and confident on a bull than on a horse and rode only bulls for the remainder of his senior year.

Richard Rigby, a high school wrestler who stood only five feet tall and weighed a mere 125 pounds, was determined to conquer a bull that weighed more than a ton. It would be a greater challenge than he had ever faced in a wrestling match. Next to any of his wrestling opponents, the bull was a monster.

"Getting down on that bull, I began to feel a lot of uncertainty," Richard said. "I began to wonder what was going to happen. His horns went straight out. The adrenalin began to really get me going. As we left the chute, he sucked my bull rope up tight, and I suddenly felt the power underneath me."

Richard continued, saying, "As we came out of the chute, he ran to the middle of the arena. Then he made a turn, and I went off. Leaving my imprint there in the dirt, he simply walked away. Val, Clint, and Jerry got me riding bulls, but you made it fun"

When I asked Richard if he'd ever considered riding a bucking horse, he said, "No, I had a hard enough time staying on a bull. I felt a horse was too far above the ground, and that would be too far for me to fall."

Dean Daniels was another SideKick who enjoyed riding bulls. Climbing on Holy Poke, he hunkered down and nodded for the gate. This Slash C Rodeo brown-and-white bull came out of the chute kicking high in the air. It was obvious that bull was not going to hold back for anybody. He had one goal in mind: to get Dean off its back. As Holy Poke turned away from Dean's hand, making for an even more difficult ride, both rider and bull remained aggressive. Then Dean's free arm got behind him, causing first his seat and then his feet to shift. With no feet, he soon lost his seat. The clock stopped when his hand left its grip on his bull rope about six seconds into his ride.

Two bulls chosen for the National Finals Rodeo in Oklahoma City were among the stock provided by Slash C. These bulls, including the one-time great bucking bull Rodeo Red, had been purchased from Neal Gay of Mesquite, Texas. Rusty drew Rodeo Red, the very bull on which PRCA bull-rider Don Gay had won a World Bull Riding Championship. Rusty knew he had a good draw, and I knew we had a good bullfighter.

After getting himself all pumped up, Rusty climbed down on the renowned bull. When the gate opened, it was obvious Rusty was holding on to a lot of bull. As they entered the arena, Rusty had just one goal: an eight-second ride followed by a safe escape.

Rusty continued to bear down hard through a move to the left, a move to the right, and an up-and-down jump with a twisting motion. Keeping his shoulders square, Rusty used his outside foot as Rodeo Red went into a spin into his hand, and stayed aboard until the whistle blew.Rusty's score of seventy-eight gave him a first-place win, a win that had been earned in eight seconds, one jump at a time. Dean was there at the right moment to help Rusty escape after he hit the ground. Bill Crittenden said, "That was the first time I had ever seen anyone ride that bull since I had purchased him. He had probably lost a little gas in the time since Don Gay had ridden him, but he still gave Rusty a good ride."

* * *

We had an impressive 160 contestants from twenty-one clubs throughout the state competing in our two-day event. Seventeen of our own SideKicks were contestants in their second high school rodeo. Once again, however, the number of spectators in attendance was disappointing. No one from our school faculty attended; not even one administrator or school board member came out to support us. Some members of the student body were there as spectators, though, and they became our cheering section.

The SideKicks held their own as they competed with the best in the state. Rusty won third-place honors in saddle bronc riding and first in bull riding. Chief took second in bull riding, Blake ended up with third place in bareback bronc riding, and Crystal placed in barrel racing. Heidi and Ann were chosen as rodeo queen attendants. They would be joining Jon Larsen and Jimmy Christensen at state.

Crystal and Rusty, both seniors, were presented the All-Around SideKicks Cowgirl and Cowboy buckles from Ralph Pitts, who'd sponsored that award. Ralph was the grandfather of Robyn, another SideKick member, and a real estate salesman in Mount Pleasant. Rusty and Crystal earned the highest number of points on a cumulative basis. Those points were earned by placing at various high school rodeos held during the 1977–78 school year.

Crystal and Rusty graduated from high school that year, along with Tim, Casey, Shorty, and Darryl. It was bittersweet to realize that these original SideKicks would no longer be representing North Sanpete High School. Adding to that feeling was the fact that some of our other original SideKicks—Danny, Dale, Val, John, Casey B, and Robert—had graduated in earlier years.

As the original SideKicks graduated, a few of them confided that they would have preferred to stay in high school and rodeo another year. What a turnaround—some of the students who didn't want to be in school at all now didn't want to leave.

CHAPTER EIGHTEEN

Don Gay at North Sanpete High School

A Lesson Learned: Self-Confidence Builds Success and Vice Versa

I HAD TO look twice. Was that Don Gay who had just walked past me? Just to make sure, I asked the person sitting next to me. It was, indeed, Don Gay. I had run into one of the hottest superstars in rodeo because I happened to be in the right place at the right time. I decided that things seemed to happen for a reason and thought what a plus it would be to have him come to the school. I knew it was a long shot—he was at the top of his game and lived nowhere near Mount Pleasant. Was there even a chance for him to fit us into his schedule?

During the fall of 1978, the school board approved my request to attend a rodeo educational seminar in Dallas, Texas. There was a place near Dallas known as the Cowboy College. It boasted various types of rodeo practice equipment, including a mechanical bull that put El Toro to shame. A lot of money and time had been put into their machine; it was the closest you could get to riding a real bucking bull.

The three days I spent at the Cowboy College educated me as to why some succeeded in competition while others didn't. Cowboys from throughout Texas were in attendance, and I became acquainted with a few who were enrolled at Sul Ross University in the West Texas community of Alpine. Sul Rose had been noted for its intercollegiate rodeo program, even claiming college rodeo had its beginnings there.

One of the most fascinating things I learned at the Cowboy College was what it takes to become a rodeo champion. The instructor had done interviews and studies about the making of rodeo champions and had come up with ten standout discoveries. At the top of the list was a strong belief in a supernatural being. To teach this concept, he passed around a mirror with these words written on it: *Who am I?* When they passed the mirror to me, I answered that I was a child of God. To my surprise, the same answer came from other cowboys. Since then, I have noticed more than one rodeo cowboy expressing his thanks to God out in the rodeo arena after making a safe bull or bronc ride.

That same instructor also pointed out that success in rough-stock riding is 75 percent or more mental.

While I was at the college, Don Gay came into the facility to work out on their gym equipment. It was obvious he was a champion by the way he carried himself. He appeared to be in top physical condition. I discovered that most professional rodeo cowboys find time for the gym as often as possible, and Don Gay was one of these. Professional cowboys continue to focus on aerobics as well as weight lifting to strengthen their legs in addition to their other exercise routines.

At that time, Don had earned four World Champion PRCA bull-riding championships plus the Seasonal Championship that year. The year before, he had made a ninety-seven-point ride on Oscar at the San Francisco Cow Palace. Introducing myself and considering it a privilege to meet him, I invited him to our high school to put on a bull-riding seminar. With his positive attitude, I knew the SideKicks would be in for a great experience if he could come. He said he would look at his schedule and give me a call.

Don invited me out to their arena in Mesquite—a famed, landmark rodeo facility in that part of Texas where pro rodeos were held on a regular basis. As I was leaving, I asked him what he thought about that 75 percent mental factor as it related to his success as a bull rider. He said he felt it was closer to 85 percent.

After returning home, I received a phone call from Don. He said he would work us into his schedule in late December, right after the National Rodeo Finals in Oklahoma City. I offered to pick him up at the airport in Salt Lake City and invited him to stay at our home. Imagine my amusement when, just before hanging up, he asked if we had an El Toro.

The first thing that entered my mind was how excited Shorty was going to be when he found out Don Gay was coming to North Sanpete. Shorty had always looked up to Don Gay and often mentioned his name in conversation. They were both short in stature and enjoyed the challenge of riding a bull. As we finished working out the details, I found myself becoming more and more excited. I couldn't wait to share the news with Shorty and the other SideKicks.

Later, Don Gay called and asked if there was any way he could break his commitment with us. I told him that would be his call but that there would be several mighty disappointed SideKicks. Don Gay went silent for a moment, then said, "Reed, I will be there." I thought, *That is the mark of a true champion.* Relief washed over me.

Shortly after Don's phone call, I received some bad news. Shorty had crashed his truck into a moving train that weekend.

He had been on his way home Saturday evening when he had hit the train just north of Mount Pleasant. It took rescuers five and a half hours to get him out of his damaged pickup truck and another four hours to get him into the ambulance and to the hospital in Provo. Apparently the wreck was so bad it was a wonder he'd survived.

Val and Shorty had been at John and Casey's house that evening, and not long after Shorty left they had heard the crash in the still of the night. They had a feeling Shorty might be involved, and so they hurried to the crash site. Val confirmed that there was no way Shorty should have survived.

When I was told Shorty might not even make it out of the hospital alive, my heart sank. He had split his head and also broken a bone near his left eye, close to his optic nerve. He had a broken arm and had broken the same leg he had broken on his bull ride in Ogden—and in exactly the same spot. He also had a punctured lung.

A few days later, I received word that Shorty was holding his own; it looked like he was going to survive. I called his sister, Renee, and told her that Chief and I were going to pick up Don Gay at the airport. If it was okay with her, we wanted to drop by the hospital on our way home and pay Shorty a visit. She agreed to meet us in the hospital foyer and take us to his room. After picking up Don at the airport, we headed home. As we approached Provo, I said, "Don, there is a member of our rodeo club here in the hospital. He was recently involved in an auto-train accident. The train was going about fifty miles an hour and he was going sixty. They collided, and he is in a bad way. You are his idol. He goes by the name of Shorty, and he enjoys riding bulls. Do you mind if we stop and pay him a visit?" Don eagerly consented.

Entering Shorty's room, I asked, "Shorty, do you know who this is?" He looked up, stared for a minute, and then said, "He looks like Don Gay to me." Don went over and sat by his bedside. They had a good visit that lasted for nearly half an hour.

Years later, I asked Shorty if he remembered Don Gay's visit. He said, "I remember every moment. That was awesome. I told Don Gay what caused him to get bucked off Oscar at the National Rodeo Finals that year. He agreed with me. I had seen his ride on TV, and there I was telling Don Gay what he did wrong on his ride. Imagine me telling Don Gay how to ride Oscar."

Shorty's father told us that Don Gay's visit with Shorty was the turning point in his recovery. After Don's visit, he'd started to mend.

It was a pleasant experience having Don stay at our home; he was easy to be around and made himself at home, quickly becoming like one of our family.

To have Don Gay in our rodeo gym at the high school was amazing. Don climbed on El Toro to demonstrate some moves. Putting his hand in the bull rope, he gave the nod for our controller to turn on the machine. When he did, El Toro nearly bucked the world champion bull rider into the sawdust.

"Whoa, whoa! When did you get this machine?" he asked. Ours was a newer model than the one he had in Mesquite, and it bucked differently. Apparently Don had never been on this newer version, and it had caught him off guard. Suddenly there was a lot of laughter.

On his last day with us, Don showed a film of him riding a bull. It was pitch-black in the old high school auditorium, and I was sitting next to the vice principal. Don was talking as we watched him ride a bull spinning wildly to the left. Suddenly, someone flicked on a lighter. The vice principal and I both jumped up at the same time. It was Don Gay, getting ready to light a cigarette. When he realized what he had done, he quickly put it out.

Bobby Hardman, a North Sanpete student, happened to be in the auditorium watching that film with us. Later Bobby said, "Don Gay broke another record. He not only won world championships in bull riding, but he is the first to ever light up a cigarette in the high school auditorium and get away with it."

Don told them that he got ready to mount a bull through a sequence of habits. He did things in the same order each time. That way he didn't miss anything as he prepared himself to ride. Don Gay is still classed as one of the top bull riders in the history of rodeo and is often considered the greatest bull rider of all time, with a total of eight World Champion Bull Riding titles to his credit—so the SideKicks paid attention to everything he said.

In the classroom, Don talked about how goal setting had helped him to several world championships. "If my main goal is to win the World in bull riding, I list the supporting goals that will get me there. Alongside those supporting goals, I list all the obstacles that would prevent me from obtaining those goals. If one of my supporting goals is getting money for my entry fee, I go to the stock contractor and tell him I will do anything for entry fee money—clean out his stock trailer, whatever."

That evening, we held a Christmas dinner for Don, the SideKicks, other seminar students, parents, school and district administrators, and members of the school board and their partners. All who attended that dinner were rewarded as they heard him speak. The theme of the event was, "People are champions who think and act like champions." As we listened to him speak, I envisioned him riding Oscar to that record ninety-seven-point score at the Grand National Rodeo in San Francisco. That record ride still holds as one of the highest scores in rodeo history.

"In this day and time, you are at a definite disadvantage without a diploma," Don told the audience. "Having a rodeo club in your school should make it easier for you club members to stay in school. I am impressed with the support you have for high school rodeo at this school." Don advised rodeo participants to "discover what you want in life, set goals, and then put your best foot forward and made it stick. You can do anything you want if you believe in yourself and God."

Don continued. "For my success, I surround myself with winners, think positive thoughts, set goals, and go for it. I give it 100 percent in all I do. Even above being a winner in rodeo is being a winner in life."

Don said he had participated in 171 rodeos that year, as many as five per day at times. He was considered one of a new breed in rodeo. He had established an image of being a professional athlete, a respected cowboy, and rodeo superstar. He told me that just prior to his coming to North Sanpete, he had turned down an offer to be in a movie. He felt his role in life was to build the image of the rodeo cowboy, but after reading the script he realized that his role would have been that of a barroom cowboy. That movie—*Urban Cowboy*—eventually came out on the big screen with John Travolta in the leading role.

Don Gay returned to his home in Texas sometime before Shorty was released from the hospital. I felt bad that Shorty had missed that seminar. When he got out of the hospital, it was in a wheelchair with his family and Val Lynch by his side.

Jerry commented that Don Gay's visit was a turning point for his brother Clint and for Jimmy's brother Wade Christensen, who was also a good bull rider. Don had told them that they would be fierce competitors, and they were.

John Larsen said, "On El Toro, Don Gay helped me a lot when he showed me, after running my bull rope around the back of my hand, to make a twist in my bull rope when I brought it through my hand. Since I began making that twist in my rope, it seemed to prevent me from getting hung up on my bull rides." The thought occurred to me that such a technique could have saved not only John but also Clint and Kelly from their hang-ups as well.

A twenty-four-by-thirty-two-inch photo print of Don Gay riding Oscar was presented to the SideKicks. The photo had been taken as the bull was standing on its hind feet in an almost vertical position to Don. He autographed the print with the words, *Best Wishes, SideKicks, Don Gay.*

* * *

After Don Gay's visit, the SideKicks were programmed and ready to make their third sponsored high school rodeo a success. There was excitement in the air as their rodeo had become rated as one of the top high school rodeos in the state. Slash C furnished the livestock again, giving us some great bucking stock. The rodeo was scheduled for Memorial Day weekend of 1979.

Chief drew Slash C's famed Powder Keg. Powder Keg was a bull most high school bull riders were afraid of back then. Jerry Lynch said, "I remember when Chief drew Powder Keg. He acted like he was all pumped up, but I could see he was scared to death.

Watching him come out of the chute, he looked one way as the bull went the other. He managed to hang on until the whistle blew, then he took off running before his feet hit the ground."

Laughing, Jerry continued. "We all had to look tough to show our 'man face.'"

Powder Keg gave Chief the thrill of his life at that rodeo. When all was said and done, he walked away with a third-place win.

Chief wasn't the only one who got a turn on Powder Keg. Val said, "I rode that bull for an eighty-one-point ride. Powder Keg was a bull many cowboys hated to draw. I rode him probably half a dozen times. He was a good ride for me when I managed to get the rodeo clowns to turn him right or left as he left the chute.

"When I sat up straight on that bull, kept my chest out, and pulled up on my rope as he began to spin, good things happened for me. Clint covered that bull more than once. On one occasion, after making a good ride, he said to Bill Crittenden, 'I wish I could get that bull to buck.' Clint had more raw talent when it came to bull riding than any of us."

A total of 181 contestants from twenty-six clubs entered, making for a total of 306 entries—fifty more than in the previous year. Twenty-nine of those were SideKick entries. Sadly, we still lacked the support of the students and faculty. Other than that, it was a great success. Blake took first in bareback bronc riding, with Jimmy placing second in that same event. Jon Larsen won the saddle bronc riding competition. Jon ended up in fifth in bull riding and sixth in bareback bronc riding. Heidi was chosen rodeo queen, while JoAnn was presented the Miss Horsemanship Award; Torie Poulsen, a new SideKicks member, was chosen as Miss Congeniality. Overall, the SideKicks did well among some mighty tough competition from throughout the state. What a year that was—Don Gay's visit followed by our third sponsored rodeo proved a successful, confidence-building experience for all.

CHAPTER NINETEEN

State Finals and Nationals

A Lesson Learned: Staying the Course

A ND THEN we were off to our second State Finals. I still shudder as I think about Clint Lynch's bull-riding experience on #155 that year. It seemed to go on forever, and Clint was finally thrown from when his hand wouldn't release from his bull rope. Things became ugly real quick as #155 dragged Clint around in a circle. Seconds seemed more like minutes.

The bull started flipping Clint around like a ragdoll. Then it used its horns to pick up bullfighter Jerry Hurst, the 1968 National High School Rodeo Finals champion bull rider, as he ran to help Clint, and Clint continued to be tossed around for what seemed like an eternity. Clint's hand was finally freed by Clint Downs, another bullfighter.

"Bull #155 was one of the best bucking bulls Slash C had," Val said. "He was also the most deadly with his head because he had a desire to hurt someone. Clint got tossed right out of the chute as I witnessed one of the most dangerous bull wrecks I had ever seen. However, looking on the positive side, it did make for some great action shots."

Referring to Clint's experience, Bill Crittenden said, "That was a bad situation. Sometime after that, I found that bull dead in my corral." To this day, no one knows why the bull died.

Jon drew a Kirby professional bucking bull named C9. When he gave the nod, the gate opened and Jon let his upper body take over. As that bull cranked, Jon continued to stay up on his rope, making correct moves and countermoves, putting forth his best effort to stay in rhythm. When the whistle blew, he jumped off his bull and made a quick escape as the bullfighters jumped in front of the bull to distract him, allowing Jon to get himself in a safe zone.

Jimmy drew Copenhagen, a Rockin R Rodeo bareback bronc, during the first go-round. He covered this bronc for a full eight seconds but didn't rack up enough points to place. During his second attempt, Jimmy drew Honky Tonk Angel. That bronc got into the air mighty quick and then continued with some big jumps. Jimmy continued to ride him for the full eight seconds only to learn that he had not marked the horse out at the gate.

Jon, Blake, and Lauren were at the top of their game throughout their high school rodeo career. All three of them were as tough as iron, always staying the course when it came to riding broncs and bulls. They became as consistent in winning as Roy Rogers, Gene Autry, and Hopalong Cassidy were in catching the bad guys. What a thrill it must have been for them to travel together, compete together, and remain best of friends.

This go-around, Blake had taken hold of his handle and scooted up next to his rigging, then nodded for the gate. Blake's bronc exploded out of the chute, then stood on its nose as its hind feet went six feet into the air. It stalled momentarily and even stumbled a little as it went to a quick right and an even quicker left, then bucked across the arena. But Blake remained fixed atop 1,200 pounds of pure power, strength, and speed. Not a bit user-friendly, this bronc put forth every effort to put

Blake in the dirt. Imagine riding a jackhammer, pogo-stick style, with one hand. Blake's covering his bronc for an eight-second ride made SideKicks history when he won first place in the second go-round on that bareback bronc. In the final round, Blake claimed first place again with another aggressive bronc ride, making him the top-ranking bareback bronc rider at the Utah High School Rodeo Finals in 1978.

The next morning the sun rose on a new state champion; SideKick Lauren Larsen, Jon's cousin, won the first go-round on Honky Tonk Angel, the same bronc Jimmy had ridden but which he'd missed out at the gate. Lauren took second place in the second go-round and ended up as runner-up to Blake. Blake and Lauren both had smiles on their faces as they heard the final results. The SideKicks now had two state champions on their way to the National Finals Rodeo in Huron, South Dakota (see appendix). Blake was awarded a beautiful hand-carved saddle and a plaque that would have made anyone proud. Lauren was given a buckle, along with a couple of beautiful plaques.

And soon they were off to the Finals to face a level of competition that would be the ultimate test of their mettle. The bucking pro-rodeo stock was rank. Jon, Lauren, and Blake had driven to Huron in Blake's uncle's 1972 Chevy pickup, which had a camper on it. That was where they slept—the first night at the Little America Truck Stop in Wyoming, the second at Mount Rushmore in South Dakota, and the third in Huron. Once at the finals, they hooked up with other Utahns who became like family as they looked out for each other. Blake's mother and sister-in-law soon joined them and were also quickly adopted into the "extended" family. Blake's father had been unable to break away because of work commitments.

The three quickly got caught up in the excitement along with the 1,500 other high school cowboys and cowgirls, their families, and friends who came from more than thirty states and at least a couple of provinces in Canada. Trucks, campers, and trailers of all kinds were parked close together. Noisy engines could be heard cruising through Huron's city streets at all hours of the day, and Blake remembers the sea of straw hats he saw everywhere he went. All of it was a dream come true for him.

Blake had ridden his first bull in Wellington at the tender age of thirteen. His brother Clair, who was a bull rider as well, had entered Blake in the bull-riding contest. "I couldn't believe how big that bull was," Blake remembered. "I weighed less than one hundred pounds. My bull did not have any horns, for which I was grateful. I stayed on him for seven seconds and felt that adrenalin rush. I had so much fun riding that bull that I became hooked."

Blake's first bareback bronc experience was at a high school rodeo in the old Golden Spike Coliseum in Ogden, where he took third. "Riding bareback broncs seemed to really click for me," Blake said. "It just felt natural. I hardly ever got bucked off. Riding saddle broncs was different—I was terrible at riding saddle broncs, even though I qualified for state in that event."

During his first go-round at Huron, Blake drew a bad horse and received a score of only sixty-three. He requested a reride, but the judges said no—something I felt was a borderline call. "Even though those bucking horses were selected from top producers, there are times when a good bronc just doesn't feel like putting out his best effort," Blake said. "Perhaps such was the case here."

In the second go-round, Blake earned a score of seventy-two, which put him in third place. Had he drawn a better horse in the first go-round, he likely would have been in the top twenty in that event and competed in Sunday's short go for a NHSRA World Title and a portion of the scholarships and awards up for grabs.

When I called Blake after more than three and a half decades later, I asked him where life had taken him after he'd left high school. He said he'd continued competing, served a mission for his church, and graduated from Brigham Young University with a major in finance. He and a partner now own a computer software company, where they serve car dealerships in the Salt Lake City area.

As he reminisced about his rodeo days with the SideKicks, Blake talked about how important rodeo was in his life and what lengths he would have gone to so he could compete: "At that time, I considered it an honor to be there at the National Finals. My parents were proud of me and my rodeo accomplishments. They supported me in everything I ever did in high school sports, but when it came to high school rodeo, they were reluctant. Now that they have both passed on, I guess it is fair to say that I would have forged their signatures if I had to so I could enter high school rodeos."

Blake placed second at the national high school level, but in my eyes and in his, it was a first-place experience we'll never forget. Blake showed us that champions are made from something deep inside—a desire, a dream, a vision, and tenacity in sticking to those things.

CHAPTER TWENTY

A California Bull-Riding School

A Lesson Learned: It's Possible to Steer Your Mind

W OULD YOU drive me to Gary Leffew's bull-riding school in California?" Tim asked. In response to my blank stare, Tim told me Gary was a 1970 PRCA World Champion bull riding champion. He then handed me the ad he had ripped out of a magazine. The ad said that John Gooddell was also going to teach how to braid bull ropes at the school. I knew that would be something I could pass on to other SideKicks, and so I began giving Tim's proposal some thought. We found a map of California and learned that the school was near San Luis Obispo. I'd never been there before, and it sounded interesting.

A couple of days later I gave Tim the okay. We made plans to leave right after Christmas and return on New Year's Day. That meant we wouldn't miss any school, since we'd be gone during school holidays.

My son traveled with us. I told both boys to keep their eyes peeled as we approached the top of the hill that led to Vegas and my old stomping grounds. Suddenly the city lights came into view, shining brightly in the middle of the desert. We spent the night there, and the next day, near Santa Maria, California, we found a motel near the road that led to Leffew's ranch. Several other cowboys were staying at the same motel, and early the next morning we heard, "Yahoo! It's going to be a great day today!"

We were excited as we followed those cowboys to Gary's ranch along a one-lane dirt road that wound eastward through the timber for a few miles. As we came upon a clearing among the trees, to the left side of the road we saw a small, round bull-riding arena constructed of wooden planks. Up the hill from us was his home, and to the right were several cars and trucks. As we got out of the car, we found ourselves among other cowboys anxious to learn how to ride bulls under Gary Leffew's watchful eye.

Gary made us feel welcome, and we got to know his can-do mentality. He began by telling his students that every day was a great day for singing a song, for smiling, and for riding bulls. Before long he had his students feeling like they could all become winners in bull riding.

In his younger days, Gary had been raised around cowboys but had never thought seriously about becoming one. In high school, he couldn't seem to focus on any goals until his father told him he should be a cowboy, something he thought was dumb—until he tried it. Becoming a cowboy changed him from being an introvert to being an extrovert and someone who was always ready for fun.

When it came to pain, Gary said there was no such thing as pain. He said it was all in your head. I thought about the time I'd been holding a horse for my dad as he'd nailed on a horseshoe. The horse had suddenly reared up, and its knee had connected with mine—and I'd felt pain. My doctor said he had treated several cowboy injuries during the annual PRCA Cattle Call Rodeo in Brawley, California. He told us how, as he x-rayed their injuries he often saw evidence of previous injuries that had not been treated because rodeo cowboys tended to put the pain out of their heads and let the injuries take care of themselves. Today's cowboys generally get excellent treatment, but that memory reinforced my understanding of the power of the mind.

Gary continued telling his students that by July 1972, he had won less than $1,000. During the next sixteen months, he'd won $18,000. He had a sweatshirt made that said, "I'm the Hottest Thing Going." "Other cowboys would look at me as if I had landed on my head one too many times," he told us. "I wore that shirt every time I rode a bull. Before long, cowboys were calling me Hot Man."

Throughout the week, Gary impressed upon us the importance of having a positive attitude. He introduced us to the book *Psycho Cybernetics,* by Dr. Maxwell Maltz.[7] *Psycho* refers to the mind, and *cybernetics* means steering—in other words, it talks about how to steer the mind. One concept from the book that impressed me was the fact that the mind cannot tell the difference between "a vividly imaginative experience and the real thing."

To demonstrate, Gary told us how he had found himself in a slump when it came to riding bulls. He was getting bucked off too often. So he decided to grab his fishing pole and head to the hills. There, he rode bulls in his mind. "I would visualize those bulls' moves, their sounds, and my own moves as I saw myself making a good bull ride," he explained. "When I came out of those woods, I was hot. I felt I could ride any bull."

Tim rode several bulls at Gary's school. Afterward, we would watch him ride on a six-foot screen under Gary's scrutiny. Gary would point out to Tim and the other students how they were forced off their bulls when they allowed their free arm to get behind them. He instructed them on how to use their free arm to make the right moves to keep from falling down the well—the inside of a spinning bull. "Only jump off a bull when he is moving," he continued. "Jump to the rear of the bull, away from its head."

Tim and I were impressed with Gary's school, and Tim suggested we invite Gary to put on a seminar at North Sanpete High. Gary agreed, and arrangements were made for him to come to the school for a three-day seminar the first week in April. We agreed to have bulls available for the bull riders.

Diane Clarloni Simmons, a reporter from Texas who was at Gary's school, heard us planning for the seminar and wanted to do a story about our rodeo club. The story was published in *The World of Rodeo*, a publication out of Montana, and was titled, "North Sanpete High School, Big Rodeo from a Little School."[8]

As we were about ready to head back home, Gary gave away large autographed prints of himself on an awesome bull ride. On my print he wrote: "Always remember you are the captain of your ship, the master of your destiny." The SideKick girls hung it in our classroom on our wall of fame, along with the pictures of Mickey Young and Don Gay. Gary's print served as a reminder that we are always in charge of our attitude.

CHAPTER TWENTY-ONE

Gary Leffew Visits North Sanpete High School

A Lesson Learned: Visualize Success

GARY'S VISIT began with a SideKicks banquet on March 27, 1980, where he was the guest speaker. More than sixty were in attendance, including school board members, school administrators, and parents.

The SideKick girls and Linda Larsen, an adult teaching assistant, took care of the invitations and made the table decorations—cowboys and horses made out of rope and paper. The menu consisted of turkey, potato salad, Jell-O salad, a relish plate, rolls, and cake. After the dinner, Gary talked to those in attendance about the importance of having a positive attitude. "When you get up in the morning, shout, 'It's a great day!'" he told us—his way of starting every day.

Gary also talked about how he had won the World Championship in bull riding in 1970. He then explained that he and his wife, along with their three children, hold ten rodeo schools each year on their sixty-two-acre ranch. He told how he had become involved in making TV commercials for trucks, airlines, and watches. He also told us how he'd actually worn a wristwatch as he'd ridden a bull in one of his commercials and how, after the bull ride, the watch had kept ticking.

Gary conducted a three-day bull-riding school in the Mount Pleasant arena, where he gave instruction on correct bull-riding fundamentals. The arena was covered with snow and the ground was frozen, but no one seemed to mind. Each rider at the seminar was videotaped on practice bulls we had leased from Slash C; the Crittendens were always there for us when we needed bucking stock. Student mistakes and merits were pointed out immediately after the ride on the instant replay. By the end of the third day, each student knew what had gone wrong with a bull ride even before viewing it on the TV screen. "Stay up on your rope," he emphasized. "Use your outside foot to pick up a point or two during a spin. Don't get sucked into the well." Not only did Gary Leffew help his students with bull-riding technique, but he also helped all of us to be more positive. Winners in the contest at the end of the seminar included a bull rider from Tooele who took first place. SideKicks club president Chief placed second, and Tim took third-place honors.

Gary Leffew inspired several SideKicks' careers. After Gary's seminar in Mount Pleasant, some SideKicks later attended his bull-riding school in California. David Breaux, John Larsen, and Dean Daniels traveled to Gary's ranch in Dean's pickup truck after Christmas that same year. Dean said he rode fifteen more bulls than anyone else at the school, but the greatest thing he got from Gary, again, was that a positive attitude made all the difference. It was more of a lesson in life than in riding bulls.

* * *

Recently, we sponsored a bucking-bull contest at Mount Pleasant's new indoor arena. Breeders of bucking bulls transported their bulls from as far away as Hawaii. I was amazed at how the bulls performed. Most of the riders were thrown within five seconds; it would have been easier to ride a skateboard up a graveled hill in a blizzard than to stay on some of those bulls for eight seconds. When I mentioned to Dean that I couldn't imagine anyone being able to ride some of those bulls for eight seconds, he demonstrated the kind of positive attitude we'd learned when he said, "There is no bull that can't be ridden."

Gary taught us how to visualize success in our minds. He helped bull riders to see themselves making successful rides and to think positive and believe in themselves. I have since seen many a bull rider ride an "unrideable" bull.

The concept of visualizing success has had a lasting effect on my life, Tim's life, and the lives of the other SideKicks who heard him teach. When I first arrived at North Sanpete High School, few if any of the SideKicks had even considered visualizing success in their lives. Their main goal was to simply make it through another day. Now they were beginning to see an amazing future as they experienced renewed self-confidence and hope.

CHAPTER TWENTY-TWO

Sponsoring Our Fourth High School Rodeo

A Lesson Learned: Resilience

EVERYONE WAS afraid to draw Power Keg at our fourth sponsored high school rodeo—everyone except Val, Chief, and Clint. Then we watched as David Breaux, a new SideKick, drew him.

"I am not going to get on that damn bull," he shouted. "And they can keep my money." So we let him draw again. This time he drew #76. David said, "I was more scared on that bull than I was when I rode my first bronc. That bull was so intimidating. He had a bad set of horns, and I was afraid I was going to be thrown right into them. I didn't stay aboard very long. In fact, it was a rather short ride."

Gary Leffew had left Chief excited about riding another bull, and he drew a Slash C by the name of Paleface. When his black Stetson made the nod, the gate swung open and Paleface came out of the chute like air coming out of a balloon. Hanging on for dear life, Chief stuck to Paleface like butter on a roll. After a wild performance, he hung on until the whistle blew. When Chief decided it was time to let go, his bull went one way and Chief took off running the other.

After Chief's ride, Dean Daniels rode a bull that put him in fifth place. Dean later told me, "That was one mean bull. He would flip his head and get his horn under your knee and just flip you off. That is probably the reason I placed on that bull—I was too scared to fall off. After the whistle blew, he threw me so high I could have grabbed on to rafters had there been any."

Slash C had arranged for professional bullfighter and rodeo clown Dean Steed to join us again. Backing Dean were bullfighters Kevin Higley and Val—our levelheaded, fearless original SideKick who showed up to fight bulls and entertain the crowd as a rodeo clown. I hadn't seen him since he had graduated.

When Val approached me out in the arena dressed as a rodeo clown, it took me back to when I'd wanted to be a rodeo clown. When I was five, my family and I went to the Ute Stampede Pro Rodeo. After watching the clown acts, I decided I was going to train my father's male goat to perform tricks. Persuading him to stand still, I would crawl under him. I thought that was cool until he decided to pee while I was crawling between his front and back legs. That ended my desire to be a goat trainer or a rodeo clown, and the goat went back to eating weeds around our homestead.

Val and I had smiles on our faces as we greeted each other that day. He looked like he was the real deal, and it felt good to have him back in the arena. He courageously fought those bulls, keeping many riders from being injured. High school rodeo had taught Val not to let fear get in the way of doing what he wanted to do on any chosen day. Beginning in Moab, Val began conquering fear with that first bareback ride, which eventually led him to riding saddle broncs and bulls, further building his self-confidence and courage. As he continues his journey in the arena of life, I know those experiences will have a positive effect on everything he does.

As I think about Val performing on the arena floor, one act in particular stands out in my mind. Tim and I laughed as we watched Val set up this gig. He told this bull rider to pretend he was hurt once he knew he was safe after his bull ride. He asked another person to pretend he was a doctor. When the bull rider began to fake being hurt, a spectator jumped over the fence and began offering his help, saying he was a real doctor. Val then had to tell him it was all an act—and it turned out to be funnier than he ever imagined. Why? The person who'd jumped over the fence was part of Val's gig but had not known the plan.

The whole thing mimicked something that had actually happened during Val's senior year. He'd been bucked off a bronc and kicked in the head and shoulder; his head was not injured, but the horse did injure his shoulder. Val's family doctor was sitting with the spectators when it happened. He jumped over the fence and came to the rescue before Val was loaded in the ambulance and taken to the hospital.

* * *

Not long after our fourth sponsored rodeo, I heard that our bullfighter Dean Steed had been seriously injured while working at a Slash C Rodeo in Hyrum. A bull had hit him in the back and broken his neck. Val was fighting bulls with Dean when it happened and reported that Dean had been punched pretty hard. Dean came home from the hospital in a wheelchair and filed a lawsuit.

Bill Crittenden related, "That incident ended up in a ten-million-dollar lawsuit against Slash C Rodeo Company. The lawsuit went on for a couple of years. Eventually, we won the case, but it was all a bad deal." Val continued fighting bulls for Bill, but it was hard being short a talented bull rider like Dean.

The news of Dean's accident hit me hard because it reminded me of an accident involving my sister. Nearly fifteen years earlier, my two sisters were on their way to my wedding reception in Wales, Utah, when they hit black ice in Nephi Canyon. I spent many hours with my younger sister, Marlene, in a Salt Lake City hospital. After getting out of the hospital, she spent the rest of her life in a wheelchair, paralyzed. Amazingly, Marlene maintained a positive attitude as she and her husband reared their two children. I hoped Dean would have as much success in life as she'd had in spite of her condition.

* * *

By the time our fourth SideKicks' sponsored high school rodeo ended, one and a half years had passed since Shorty's auto-train accident. As the annual Pioneer Days Rodeo approached, Shorty decided he would enter the bull-riding competition. This celebration was being held in his hometown of Fairview, a close-knit community with a population of 1,247—at least that's what the sign says as you enter town.

Many in Fairview knew Shorty as a friend and neighbor, and several in the community had followed him in his rodeo activities prior to his accident. They'd felt his pain when he was in that terrible accident.

At the Pioneer Days Rodeo, Shorty's father was sitting in the bleachers among a sellout crowd, not knowing that Shorty had entered the bull-riding event. Shorty says he began to think about what his father would be going through when he found out. He would undoubtedly be tense, nervous, excited, hopeful, and scared when he heard the announcer say, "The next bull rider is a hometown cowboy, Glen Terry, better known as Shorty."

Shorty's mother refused to watch him ride. "I began to feel her concerns as I walked down to the arena with my rodeo gear in hand," he said. "When the announcer mentioned the next bull rider was me, the crowd exploded. Coming out of the chute on a bull called #76, I heard screaming and hollering throughout my ride. There was so much noise I couldn't even hear the whistle blow."

Recalling the ride, Jerry Lynch said, "I was there and saw it all happen. That rodeo crowd became totally ecstatic. Even Bill Crittenden, who seemed to enjoy watching riders being thrown from his bucking stock, was rooting for Shorty. It was obvious Bill was hoping along with the rest of us that Shorty would ride that Slash C bull for the full eight seconds."

"I felt for Shorty," Bill said. "I had visited with him when he was in the hospital. This bull was no joyride—#76 had a set of horns that came out of his head upward. I called them devil horns. Shorty made a beautiful ride on that bull. He even stuck some iron into that bull during his ride."

After Shorty had covered his bull for the full eight seconds, he heard a deafening uproar from the spectators. He ended up splitting first place with another bull rider. "It was an experience I will never forget," Shorty later said to me. "After that bull ride, I sold my bull ropes—even sold the one you taught me how to braid in high school—so I would never be tempted to ride another bull." Later, his father, Ross, told me, "I was so glad when Shorty got rid of those damn bull ropes."

Shorty's ability to come back and fight his fears was evidence of his mental toughness. The definition of toughness doesn't involve physical strength or size but being able to withstand something without showing weakness. Shorty showed toughness through his comeback. He faced every challenge head-on as he remained honest to himself and his wellness. To do what he did at the Fairview Pioneer Days Rodeo took incredible strength and resilience.

* * *

At the beginning of that next school year, we had a major setback that tested our mettle. A student had asked if he could borrow the club's bronc saddle. Since we had purchased it for our student body, I gladly said yes. Later, another SideKicks member asked if he could borrow the same bronc saddle, as he had entered a rodeo in the saddle bronc competition. When I contacted the first student to get the saddle back, he told me he had given it to his cousin in Neola.

While at a team-roping jackpot in Neola, I met this cousin and asked him if I could pick it up. He had been told not to give it to me.

Returning home, I reported it to school authorities, who reported it to the police. The police called the sheriff's department in Duchesne County. Their sheriff apparently went to the house, saw the saddle in the garage, and noticed that it had *NS SideKicks* engraved on the fenders, but his hands were tied since it was a civil matter. Not even our school superintendent could help us retrieve the SideKicks' bronc saddle.

As far as I was concerned, that saddle was stolen from us. It was a huge disappointment, but we didn't let it get us down too long. It was a great opportunity for the SideKicks to learn to move forward and to be resilient even in the face of tough times.

CHAPTER TWENTY-THREE

"Ma"

A Lesson Learned: A Mother Can Have Great Impact on Young Lives

As I think back on that stolen saddle, I think back on three of the SideKicks who had often ridden it—Val, Wade, and Jerry. And I can't help remembering their sweet mother, Arlene. She was a great support not only to her boys but to the other SideKicks, who all called her Ma.

Arlene Emmett became the SideKicks' advisor when Clint was elected club president. Today she is buried next to Clint in the Mount Pleasant City Cemetery. A horse and colt are engraved on her tombstone, along with the names of her children: Val, Clint, Wade, Jerry, and Becky.

A solemn spirit attended her funeral, much as one would expect. Jerry had asked if I would say a few words, something I considered a real honor. The funeral was held in the church on State Street—the "yellow church," as locals call it, the one without a steeple. Sitting at the back of the chapel was Bill Crittenden of Slash C Rodeo Company. He had driven some distance to show his respect for this rodeo mom. I didn't recognize him without his cowboy hat until he came up to me and said hello. Bill had befriended the Lynch boys, even putting some of them on his payroll. They, in turn with the other SideKicks, considered him a close friend.

In life, Arlene could usually be found in the announcer's booth lending a hand during each SideKicks rodeo and seminar. Her boys always knew she was there for them.

At one Lehi High School Rodeo, Jerry, her youngest son, came out on a bareback bronc and was really getting yanked around. He was thrown, landing hard in the dirt. When he got up on his feet, I saw him holding his wrist against his chest with an expression of pain on his face. As I ran over to him, the ambulance entered the arena. Keeping his arm against his chest, Jerry kept repeating, "My ribs, my ribs." I thought, *Oh, this could be really bad.*

Suddenly Jerry's mother came into the arena. I approached her and told her Jerry appeared to have injured his ribs. She got in the ambulance and rode with him to the hospital. Later I learned he was saying *wrist,* not *ribs;* he had fractured his wrist.

Later, we were at the Huntington rodeo when Val came off his bronc and was injured. He had been thrown over the head of his horse and had hit a cement wall; after that he didn't remember much. I recall driving him to the nearest hospital in Price, some twenty miles to the north. When the X-ray came back, the doctor informed us that Val had broken his left wrist. Since it was an injury to a joint, they couldn't do anything for him there. We were told he had to be taken to Payson in the morning.

We drove the approximately seventy miles back to Mount Pleasant, and then he and Arlene drove another sixty to Payson the next morning. I could tell Val was hurting as we traveled that first leg—in fact, he let me know he was hurting every time I hit a bump in the road. We finally arrived at his house a little after midnight.

Val said, "When we got home, my mother made me a bed on the couch. She slept in a chair next to me. When the sun came up the next morning, she was there for me. My mother never got mad at me for getting hurt; she only got mad at me for not trying. That morning she told me I just needed to learn how those horses were."

Under similar circumstances, most mothers would have banned rodeo. Not Arlene. She continued to be our club's most supportive mother—and her sons' greatest inspiration. Her home was always open to the SideKicks and their rodeo buddies. Coming home from a rodeo late at night, you could often find high school rodeo cowboys sleeping wherever they could find a spot. In the morning, whatever she was able to gather up for breakfast was made available to everyone. That little white, wood-framed house on State Street became everyone's home away from home.

Many of the SideKicks shared their thoughts about her at the funeral. She'd filled an empty spot in Casey's and John's lives. She had been Kevin's strength. Shorty said, "She was always there for us." Dean Daniels reminisced about the photo album he'd once given her, its cover made out of leather hand embossed with the words *World's Greatest Rodeo Mom. Thanks, Ma. We love you.*

No one was ever turned away from the SideKicks; we accepted everyone, and so did Arlene. She may not have had much to give in terms of material goods, but she gave all she had to her children and to those SideKicks. And what she gave made a big impact in their lives, never to be forgotten.

CHAPTER TWENTY-FOUR

High School Rodeo Continues to Deliver

A Lesson Learned: Success Breeds Success

A Natural High

SideKicks gathered up
In an old station wagon
Sided by a pickup truck
For their first rodeo.
Butterflies in stomachs
Flying faster
Taking a drink
Of adrenalin.
As they sat down
On the back of dynamite.
One by one nodded
As the gate swung wide
Unleashing an overdose
Of a natural high
That has carried them
Through a lifetime.

—Jerald King

We all had mixed emotions when the decision came to remove rodeo from North Sanpete High School. During the 1980–81 school year, the administration decided to put the high school rodeo program in the hands of the parents, mostly because of school insurance issues and liabilities.

The school gave El Toro to Snow College with the agreement that the SideKicks could use it whenever they wanted. However, El Toro had already worn itself out. A few SideKicks went down to Snow College a couple of times to see if they could squeeze another ride out of their old mechanical bucking machine, but it was useless. Whatever happened to El Toro after that remains a mystery.

Management of high school rodeo was and is much different than with other athletic organizations. Today high school rodeo is managed by parents; State Athletic Association programs are managed by educators. High school rodeo has statewide boundaries, with rodeo finals at a national level; high school athletes compete at the region level before qualifying for state. Most of all, high school rodeo is not sanctioned by the State High School Athletic Activities Association.

For high school rodeo to have been supported by the North Sanpete School District during those six years, where high school sports ruled, leaves me in awe. North Sanpete High School rodeo had provided positive direction in the lives of many of its students. It had given them unforgettable experiences and opened doors where there had been walls. The kids would never have experienced the natural highs they did had they only been given the opportunity to watch others being involved as they sat on the sidelines.

In the 1980 North Sanpete High School yearbook, a full page was devoted to the High School Rodeo Club, featuring rodeo club members. And rodeo club president Chief was also featured on another page as a member of the student council.

The natural highs we all experienced through rodeo remain unforgettable.

* * *

During the eighties, Lewis Fields and Mickey Young were the only two Utahns to represent their state with high rankings in the Professional Rodeo Cowboys Association. Prior to that, it was only Lane Frost's father, Clyde. In 2013, there were several contenders from Utah who were in the top twenty spots of professional rodeo. Some of their success can be attributed in part to high school rodeo since several of them began their rodeo careers as members of the National High School Rodeo Association.

Driving into Milford, Utah, through any of its three entrances, you'll see a sign that reads, "Welcome to Milford, the Home of World Champion Saddle Bronc Rider Cody Wright." Other Wright names have been added to the sign to honor their accomplishments in professional rodeo. Bigger signs will be necessary as the success stories continue.

On several occasions I witnessed Cody leaving a high school rodeo with the All-Around Award. In 2014, his son Rusty became a two-time National High School Saddle Bronc Riding Champion. That same year he also became the Utah State High School saddle bronc champion with his younger brother Ryder trailing as runner-up in that event. Ryder was also the National Junior High School bull-riding champion at the time.

The story continues with Cody's brothers. Jake won the National High School Finals Saddle Bronc Championship in 2007, and Spencer won the same honor in 2008. Jesse, Jake's twin brother, became the current PRCA world champion saddle bronc rider in the Professional Rodeo Cowboys Association, and Jesse was runner-up the following year. At the time of this writing, Cody was currently leading in the PRCA saddle bronc standing for 2014.

On July 24, I watched the Wright brothers compete against each other in the saddle bronc competition in Spanish Fork, Utah. At the age of eighteen, Rusty ended up leading the pack during that evening's performance.

When Evelyn Wright signed the permission slip for her oldest son's first entry, she couldn't foresee the rough-stock juggernaut she and her husband Bill had turned loose on the world. "I had no idea it would go this far," Evelyn said. "They love it and they are good at it."

Their mother continued. "As the two older boys began roping in high school rodeos, the cost of hauling horses and paying entry fees became too much. We told the boys they were going to have to ride rough stock because we couldn't haul the horses long distances. So they all became bronc riders and went on to become champions."[9]

During the National Finals Rodeo in December 2014, four of the Wright brothers competed in saddle bronc riding. The youngest of the four, Spencer, came into the finals in nearly last place, number eleven out of the top fifteen. But at the end of the ten days of competition, he ended up first in the average and first in the world for that year.

Other writers could gloat about cowboys and cowgirls who have been involved in high school rodeo in their states—even in Canada and Australia—and then went on to make it big in the pros. High school rodeo provides opportunities for individuals from all walks of life to continue to excel beyond high school.

Attending the State High School Rodeo Finals in Heber, Utah, June 4–7, 2014, was a highlight of my life. I witnessed twenty-four clubs participating, with approximately 550 high school students from Utah. Even though Sanpete County, home of the SideKicks, was without a club, it was exciting to watch contestants from Sanpete compete as members of other clubs. At the National High School Finals Rodeo in Rock Springs in July 2014, I witnessed something spectacular. Forty states, five Canadian provinces, and Australia made up the 12,500 membership of the National High School Rodeo Association. Fifteen hundred of those members, along with their parents and friends, were in Rock Springs for the week of July 13–19.

The performance began with three national anthems: the Canadian, the Australian, and our own "Star-Spangled Banner." Two arenas ran concurrently, with rough-stock events and goat-tying in one and timed events in the other. The activities could be seen from a large covered grandstand filled with spectators as well as on two big screens. A total of twelve performances plus the short go and the finale continued throughout the entire week. Sitting together by state, province, or country, the spectators became the cheering section for their contestants. The entertainment was nonstop. Amazing to me were the number of banners displayed spotlighting sponsors as well as the large trade show being held under several huge tents.

More than seventy rodeo personnel oversaw a large number of student volunteers; leaders from various State High School Rodeo Associations were also there to assist as needed. The rodeo program listed page after page of awards that would be handed out. Several high-school-age rodeo contestants were handed scholarships.

The year 2014 marked the tenth year of the National Junior High School Rodeo Finals. At state that year, Colton Humphries, an eighth-grade North Sanpete Middle School student, became the bull-riding state champion. His grandfather, Kelly Poulsen, was one of the original SideKicks. At the age of fifteen, Colton competed in the National Junior High School Bull Rider Championship in Des Moines, Iowa. He was featured among roughly a thousand contestants from forty-two states, five Canadian provinces, and Australia. There was more than $75,000 in prizes and more than $100,000 in college scholarships up for grabs. Colton made a great ride during the first go-round but was bucked off in the second. On July 26th of that year, he was named the world reserve champion bull rider of the National Little Britches Rodeo Association.[10]

Who does Colton thank for his bull-riding success? He expressed his gratitude to his family and former SideKick member Dean Daniels, along with Dean's son Dustin, who is a member of the PRCA and a professional bull rider. Colton said, "Without them, I would not be where I am today. I can't wait until I am eighteen and can join the professional bull riders' circuit. I look forward to the day when I can make a living riding bulls."

Another success story is that of Daylon Swearingen and his friend Hunter, who'd both traveled from Upstate New York with Daylon's mother Carrie, to Rock Springs for the finals. Hunter qualified in bull riding and Daylon in bronc and bull riding. It was pleasing to see Daylon walk away with the All-Around Rookie Championship. He later told me, "My parents own a rodeo company, but this Rock Springs experience helped me to stretch." His words reinforced what I've known all along: rodeo helps good boys to become great men. Perhaps someday these two boys will join the ranks of world champion cowboys who came up through the ranks of high school rodeo.

For me, the National High School Rodeo Finals and the stories I heard there were a testament to the impact high school rodeo can have in the lives of the youth who participate.

Looking Back and Facing Forward (2015)

A Lesson Learned: "Begin with the End in Mind"
— Stephen R. Covey[11]

Cowboy's Home

The coyotes sing on distant hills.
My mind drifts back to dusty fields
When life has me feeling mighty low.
With distant memories of a life in rodeo,
Joy fills my soul as I still hear
The national anthem.
The cowboy's prayer brings a little tear
The pain washed away
By leaders who believed in me.
I wouldn't be where I am without my past; the future brighter.
May all dusty trails bring cowboys home,
To a warm fire on a stormy night.

—Jerald King

MORE THAN FORTY YEARS have gone by since the SideKicks opened a new chapter in North Sanpete High School history. Were those efforts really worth the risks? Did rodeoing in their high school years make a difference in the lives of those students who got involved? I had a great time catching up with some of the originals not too long ago. Let's journey with them as they share what they see in their rearview mirror.

Many of the original SideKicks now have gray hair. Some of them sport salt-and-pepper beards. They look a little heavier than when I remembered them in high school. Children were calling them "grandpa" and "grandma." One thing is certain— none has been exempt from the aging process. Another thing is also certain—my memories of them have become more treasured as time has passed.

Val felt like the club changed him for good. He said, "During my junior and senior years, high school rodeo gave me a reason to stay in school. Those couple of years made a difference in the direction my life has gone. It gave me a reason to face life's challenges without fear. I quit being afraid as high school rodeo turned loose the adventurous side of me. It allowed me to grow and become the person I am today.

"You helped me as we interacted together," Val continued as he looked at me. "You and that high school rodeo experience shaped the life I enjoy today—a good wife, a married thirty-four-year-old daughter, a seven-year-old grandchild, and a good job. High school rodeo did it for me. It gave me confidence, providing me with a path of understanding that I could do anything I want. There is nothing one can't do if they will just try. Nine times out of ten it will work in their favor."

"Val got into wrestling first while in high school," said Wade, chiming in. "Then came high school rodeo. More than anything, rodeo seemed to help Val build his self-confidence and self-esteem. In fact, it built my self-esteem too. My self-confidence continued to grow as I became more involved with high school rodeo."

Val continued. "Rough-stock rodeo was like living on the edge. It made wrestling look like a picnic." When I asked him what had made him want to participate in all three rough-stock events, he said, "It was because of the rush it gave me. It was so fun, and I loved the challenge. I really wanted to get good at what I was doing. I was experiencing a whole new world with high school rodeo. I was enjoying the challenge of drawing the rankest stock and winning. High school rodeo became a drug. I had to be involved."

Dean Barney, a lifelong resident of this area, said, "That North Sanpete High School Rodeo program helped a lot of kids. I have heard several mention the value that program has had in their lives. I wish I could have had that kind of opportunity when I attended high school at North Sanpete."

"What a blessing that rodeo program was for us. Reed, you can't imagine the impact it has had on lives," Tim affirmed.

John then said, "That is the only reason I graduated from high school."

"We had so much fun," Jerry commented. "High school rodeo never gave me a bad experience. Even when I got hurt, it was not a bad experience. The thing that stands out in my mind coming from that experience was the camaraderie, the friendships we made with each other. We worked together and we helped each other. Often times it was with nothing more than a box of saltine crackers and two dollars in our pocket."

"That Moab trip sure was fun," Shorty said, turning to me. "Of those high school rodeo memories, some were good and some were bad. Being voted president of the SideKicks and you teaching me how to braid bull ropes were good experiences. And bad? In Hurricane, I qualified for state on

Willy only to have a bull rider complain that I had my sleeve rolled up. That disqualified me, allowing him to take my slot, and it took away my opportunity to go to state. I was not even aware of that rule. But I learned to stay positive through it all. You taught me the value of positive thinking. It's all in the mind," he finished. When I asked Shorty if high school rodeo was worth the risk, he replied, "Absolutely, without any reservation. That is what gave me the desire to hold on for my diploma."

Rusty agreed. "High school rodeo is the only thing that kept me in school. If not for rodeo, I would have lost interest in school. We had so much fun. The camaraderie and the friendships we made, not only within the club but throughout the state, continue even today. That experience has created some good memories for me, which linger on."

David Breaux said, "When I rode my first bareback bronc, I was scared to death. I was shaking in my boots. I even remember the name of the horse—One-Eyed Jack. He threw me off pretty quickly. I didn't even come close to marking him out. In fact, it took me nine bronc rides before I was able to mark one out. That adrenalin rush was what carried me through my high school rodeo days. I went to the State High School Rodeo Finals twice and then rodeoed for two years after I graduated from high school. In fact, it was that adrenalin rush that carried me to driving demolition cars for fourteen years and then racing cars for another twelve."

David's son Braiden took a different stance. "I prefer racing cars—at least I have a steering wheel and a brake. At least I have control over all that madness."

"My best memories were the way you helped me, teaching me to be more positive, giving me a new hold on life," Chief told me. "I was a young teenager headed down the wrong road. There was a time when I didn't even want to go to school. Building that new arena, participating in those rodeo schools, being in high school rodeos, and taking Zig Zigler's 'I Can' class all gave me a new lease on life. Without you, I probably would not have made it."

"We sure did have some fun times during those high school rodeo days," Danny offered. "That was a good experience with great memories." When I reminded Danny that he was the first SideKick to ride rough stock when he rode his first bronc horse, he nodded and said, "Yep, in Moab—Do you remember when I gave you a push up the hill with my truck?"

Two of the SideKicks are now husband and wife. JoAnn and Ted Mollinet were happy to share how being part of the club made life better for them. JoAnn mentioned how much she enjoyed Don Gay's visit when he came to the high school. "At state," she said, "I felt honored to have been chosen Miss Congeniality from among thirty-five contestants who qualified to be in the queen contest. I also loved qualifying for state in pole bending. Thanks to your good example, you gave us the push to move forward."

JoAnn's husband, Ted, added, "Those road trips were enjoyable, but to meet the challenge of climbing on a bareback bronc and feel that adrenalin rush was an unforgettable experience."

"That rodeo program was good for all of us," Kelly said. "It has made us all better people. Whenever any of us come together, those SideKicks experiences always come up. Those memories have become the highlights of our lives."

Casey B said, "I would not have traded that high school rodeo experience for anything. It kept a lot of kids out of trouble. Some of those kids were going down the wrong road. It created a new interest, something that got their attention to do good rather than bad. Even though a couple may have fallen through the cracks, it made a difference in their lives, too."

Jerry added, "That rodeo program kept a whole bunch of us in school. It gave us a purpose and made things exciting and fulfilling. It left a big imprint in my life." Suddenly he went silent, seeming deep in thought. He then said, "Without that high school rodeo program in the school, I would have been a high school dropout; I know I would have ended up in jail."

Josh Taylor joined the rodeo club later. He had never really been on a horse before he decided to climb aboard a bronc. He said, "That first trip out on my bareback bronc was like riding the scariest roller coaster in the world times two. He was so powerful I suddenly felt a natural high as it got my adrenalin going. I remember getting up out of the dirt thinking I had faced my fears. *What an accomplishment,* I thought. That ride really boosted my self-esteem. I was ready to go and do it again. After a couple of bronc rides, there have not been many things I have found myself fearing. Of my years in high school, that was the best year I ever had. I earned a 3.0 grade-point average that year."

As Val and I later talked about some of the choice memories of high school rodeo, he said, "To be one of those original SideKicks who paved the way is one of my fondest memories. We started out knowing very little about high school rodeo. We became trailblazers. Being outside the norm, we stayed focused and had direction. Mickey Young was one of our best motivators. He really helped me to understand the power of the mind.

"When we started high school rodeoing, we didn't know much about equipment, technique, or anything else. Back behind the bucking chutes, it amazed me how willing cowboys were to help and teach one another. I wrestled in high school and played all sports. If I were to ask any of those guys for help, they would have turned me down flat. Rodeo is different than any other sport I have experienced when it comes to helping one another."

* * *

Being involved in high school rodeo was life-changing for the SideKicks. Their stories and insights emphasize the importance of getting kids on the right track and what can happen if they go down the wrong road. Researchers have found that there's a widespread problem in the school system today, where people are finding themselves on the wrong road because of their choices in high school: "New research by the University of Utah underscores the importance of policies in the public education system helping students avoid dropping out of school. Research by the College of Law found that failure to graduate is a precursor to larger personal and social problems, including a higher rate of criminal activity. The combination of overly harsh school policies and the increased involvement of law enforcement in schools has created a 'school to prison pipeline' in which students are funneled toward the criminal justice system instead of higher education with the use of suspensions, expulsions and school-based arrests, the study concludes."[12]

High school students today should be experiencing what the SideKicks experienced forty years ago. How much better off would students be if they mastered the ability to take risks, to face their fears, and learn how to deal with failure? Every student should have the opportunity to belong, to experience natural highs, and to learn to be resilient. Every student should have the opportunity to set goals and to fulfill their dreams. As Ernest Hemmingway put it, "There are some things which cannot be learned quickly and time, which is all we have, must be paid heavily for their acquiring."[13]

Epilogue

Less than two years after Clint's passing, I visited with Lane Frost at the National Finals Rodeo in Las Vegas, Nevada. Lane was a Utah native who had moved with his family to Oklahoma when he was a freshman. I remembered him as a small-framed cowboy with a readymade smile who seemed to be an exact replica of Clint Lynch.

Lane's mother, Elsie, talked about Lane at a cowboy church service one beautiful Sunday morning at Frontier Park during the Cheyenne Frontier Days Celebration. She told a large gathering that Lane had struggled in school with dyslexia.

But you would never have known Lane had any disabilities. He won the National High School Rodeo Finals Bull Riding Championship in 1981. Then he went on to win the National Finals Rodeo average in 1986 and the PRCA World Bull Riding Championship in 1987. In 1988, he rode Red Rock on the last night of the Challenge of Champions in Spanish Fork, Utah and won the contest.

After Spanish Fork, Red Rock was retired from pro rodeo. Until Lane's nine-second ride, the bull had been unridden. Clint had demonstrated a similar kind of ability on Powder Keg at the high school level. Many felt that if Clint had wanted to achieve in bull riding as much as Lane had, Clint could have gone to a much higher level in that event.

Like Clint, Lane was taken from us at an early age. It happened while Lane was riding a bull named Taking Care of Business in the Cheyenne Frontier Days Rodeo. On July 30, 1989, after completing a ninety-two-point ride, Lane dismounted and landed in the mud. The bull turned and hit him in the side with his horn, breaking Lane's ribs and severing a main artery. Lane started running toward the bucking chute, and as he was motioning for help, he collapsed. Lane died on the arena floor from excessive bleeding before he could be transported to the hospital.

I still feel a loss over both their deaths.

Nearly eighteen years have passed since Clint's funeral. While I was getting a haircut one day, Clint's sister-in-law Jill walked into the room, and I was able to ask her how Clint's family was doing. She assured me that they were all grown and that they'd turned out well. "At least I think so," she concluded.

At the age of fifty-four, Val has earned two associate degrees and a bachelor's degree in business and operational health and safety. He is currently manager for a health-and-safety program in New Mexico. His brothers Wade and Jerry also have good jobs in the coal mining industry.

John, Casey, and Tim Larsen each had dreams to fulfill. After high school, John gave up bull riding and put together a sheep operation. He also became a heavy equipment operator. He was fulfilling his dreams when he rolled his pickup, an accident that left him physically handicapped. Today, however, he continues to utilize the winning attitude he learned while riding bulls.

Casey joined the Marines and rode bareback bronc horses on the Marine rodeo circuit. After an honorable discharge, he joined the Professional Rodeo Cowboys Association, riding broncs with the best in the business. He qualified for the Wilderness Circuit Finals twice. He is the real deal, representing his family as a third-generation bronc rider.

As I was sitting in the grandstand at the 2014 Pendleton Roundup in Pendleton, Oregon, one of the oldest and finest rodeos in the world, I watched Casey and his grandfather, Chris—with half a century between their ages—each riding a bronc horse. I imagined Casey riding a bareback bronc in the eighties and his grandfather riding a saddle bronc in that same arena in the thirties.

Casey built a nice log home outside of town, a real contrast from the home in which he grew up. He and his wife owned Casey's City Lunch Café in Mount Pleasant for years while he operated his own trucking business. His two sons and two daughters have now given him grandsons and granddaughters to enjoy.

Rusty Bench gave up riding bulls after he graduated from high school but continued riding saddle broncs until he was twenty-eight. He said, "Today I feel a few pains from my rodeo participation. However, the memories, experiences, and fun are well worth the pain. My only regret is I didn't get on more broncs." Rusty continues to entertain many with his musical talents. His daughter, her husband, and their family are my neighbors and do the things that make our area a good place in which to live. Rusty makes his living repairing air compression equipment.

Tim gave up bull riding after high school, became a truck driver, and then landed a good job that took him to several parts of the United States. Finally, he was able to settle down and fulfill his dream. He and his wife now own and operate a registered Angus cattle business and have made a comfortable life for themselves as they too enjoy their grandchildren.

After graduating from high school, Shane "Chief" Walters continued riding bulls in the Rocky Mountain Rodeo Association, now known as the Rocky Mountain Professional Rodeo Association; it sponsors thirty-seven rodeos in the Intermountain area. After completing basic training in New Jersey, Chief ended up in the Airborne unit in South Korea and Germany as an airplane mechanic. Before long he found himself jumping out of airplanes over San Salvador with a toolbox in his hand. Today he enjoys spending time with his sons on the reservation and cares for his ailing father.

After he graduated from North Sanpete High School, Richard Rigby served his country for twenty-six years in the Army National Guard. He even spent time in Germany with Val and Jerry and later in Bagdad as a staff sergeant. He currently works for the coal industry in our area.

Glen Terry, aka Shorty, has a loving wife and a good job at the Farmers Insurance headquarters in Pocatello, Idaho, where he works in maintenance. He describes his life as "great." One can't know Shorty today without being moved by his attitude toward life, marriage, and family. His SideKicks memories remain an important part of his life.

Darryl Peel earned his associate's degree and became a real estate salesperson. Currently he is also a licensed building contractor, working mostly on commercial building projects. He spent seventeen years building the beautiful home in which he and his family now live.

Dale Peel graduated with a university degree in art education. We even spent time together teaching at North Sanpete High School. He now owns and operates his own company, Peel Furniture Works, and specializes in the making of pioneer furnishings.

Dean Daniels makes a living operating heavy equipment. On the side, he raises bucking bulls for pro rodeo. With pride in his voice, he said, "One of my bulls was ridden only one time in three years." As he showed me the video, it was easy to see why.

Jon Larsen has taken over the family ranch, while his cousin Lauren has vanished. No one knows where he is. Some say he is in the Secret Service.

Kelly Poulsen is a heavy equipment operator. He also remains a cowboy poet.

Blake Nielsen, a graduate of Brigham Young University, makes a living with the computer skills he mastered at BYU.

After Wade Christensen, Jimmy's brother, had qualified for the Wilderness Circuit Finals eight times riding bulls in Pro rodeo, I lost track of him. It was good to see him again at the group photo along with their sister. Those thirty five years had passed by quickly.

David Breaux owns and operates his own business in town.

Robert Draper was disabled in an automobile accident, and now calls Oklahoma his home.

Casey Blackburn works for the oil industry.

Danny Livingston is involved in the livestock industry.

Kevin Thompson remains employed out of the area.

Jimmy Christensen works for the turkey industry in the area.

The following poem is dedicated to the SideKicks and others who served our country. Their service is much appreciated.

Lariats of Freedom

As saddles are set and cattle shuffled in,
Let's take a moment to cover hearts.
Giving thanks to all soldiers,
Past and present.
With the snap of every chute, the burst of speed.
As loops fall freely
Around horns of opposition,
And heels are gathered up

Stretching in a team.
As flags are waved,
Let's remember lariats of freedom
Thrown from soldiers gathering tyrants,
Ready to horn freedom
Dallied to the American saddle of passion and pride.
As we play, let's give thanks
For all who fought
For lariats of freedom
Thrown today.

—Jerald King

Afterword

A student who is unmotivated with school can become difficult. With a little innovating thinking, a difficult student can be transformed into a contributing citizen.

With the SideKicks, high school rodeo created a desire to experience a cowboy way of life. My father had only a fifth-grade education, but his teachings allowed me to capture student interest and gave me a way to promote fun within my classroom.

What will work for other teachers and schools who are open to innovation is another story in the making, but as this *Deseret News* article testifies, it's vital to think outside the box:

In discussions about how to achieve excellence in public education, a recurring theme centers on the need to create a culture of innovation. But innovation requires thinking outside of the so-called box, and the box that is the public school system is solidly fortified by centuries of tradition. . . .

What policy leaders and lawmakers need to assess is how much control they are willing to give up in order to give sufficient latitude to teachers and administrators to take risks. . . .
They need to accept the fact that innovation rarely comes

*from the top down and can't thrive in a system that
remains boxed in by tradition.*[14]

As today's schools become more focused on test scores, school grades, and the common core to the exclusion of student innovation, the risk of fewer and fewer students being able to experience natural highs, peer connections, and enjoyment in their school settings increases. For a significant number of students who lack any outlet, interest in school often wanes, and dropout rates escalate. Depression and discouragement even lead some to suicide.

Research has shown that being poor can adversely affect the brain because there is less stimulation and fewer growth opportunities. According to research, the condition of poverty led to a mental burden akin to losing 13 IQ points.[15] The number of people living in poverty in the United States is 46.5 million. In addition, about 31 percent of Americans in poverty have been diagnosed with depression, twice the ratio of those not in poverty, according to a Gallup poll.[16] This should raise a few red flags in our educational focus. Some of the original SideKicks grew up in poverty. With high school rodeo, poverty no longer seemed a limitation as this innovation opened up new growth opportunities and gave certain Side-Kicks a new hold on life.

A *Deseret News* clipping cites a study where researchers discovered that technology was not the silver bullet for poverty. Similarly, a study published by the *American Economic Journal* revealed that computer ownership had "no effects on any educational outcomes, including grades, test scores, credits earned, attendance, and disciplinary actions. In other words, having a computer didn't really help kids from low-income families do better in school."[17]

High school rodeo provided an incentive for North Sanpete High School students who would not otherwise have done so to buckle down and earn a diploma. And a diploma, of course, led to better employment opportunities, resulting in more dreams being fulfilled, increased stability in family life, and an overall improved satisfaction in life.

By learning how to be resilient, to endure pain, and too use pain as fuel to move forward, the SideKicks as adults have been able to move forward when hit with obstacles such as divorce, unemployment, and addiction. They acquired the tools to convert life's setbacks into successes. Even those SideKicks who had to deal with learning challenges discovered how to compensate, remain positive, and stay focused as they continued along the trail of life. High school rodeo gave them a mindset to make the most out of opportunities in spite of the obstacles thrown in their path. They learned how to face their fears. As they looked fear in the eye and took on risks, more opportunities opened up, helping them move forward instead of backing down in difficult times. Those traits have a ripple effect within their families today.

Some SideKicks have done better in life than they would have had they pursued a college degree. Although those degrees make a huge difference in many cases, there are times when they do not: "In 2012, a whopping 44 percent of recent college graduates were 'unemployed', meaning they were holding jobs that did not require a bachelor's degree, according to a report by the Federal Reserve Bank of New York."[18]

Part of the success of the SideKicks is due to their active participation in something worthwhile. "Extracurricular activities [provide] many student growth opportunities. Schools should leave no student on the outside looking in. One will never catch a fish if they don't put a line, hook, and bait in the water. No one can reach a goal unless they actually do something. 100% of opportunities are lost when a student is never invited to participate."[19]

There seems to be an alarming trend for educators today to focus on test scores, grades, and other statistics and to discount the value of extracurricular activities. We can learn much from the past. Life can often be best understood by looking backward, at what worked and what didn't, but then it becomes important to live our lives looking forward.

I asked myself so many times if the risks associated with high school rodeo were worth it for those original Side Kicks. Their adventures included injuries. However, when the big picture came into view, the ratio between the numbers of bronc and bull rides verses the numbers of injuries among remained small. What those students got out of rodeo was invaluable.

Football and high school rodeo will always present risk of injury, but improvements have been made. Rodeo has developed a helmet to prevent head injuries for bull riders and protective vests for rough-stock riders. In addition, bareback rigging has been improved.

The benefits of both high sports continue to produce positive outcomes among our youth in spite of the risks involved. However, the risks do remain greater with rodeo than football. "According to a 2009 study by the University of Calgary in Alberta, Canada, rodeo's rate of catastrophic [permanent] injuries was 9.45 per 100,000 athletics from 1989 to 2009 , compared to football's 0.8. This spanned all contestants in rough stock, timed events and barrel racing, but bull riders topped the charts."[20]

But what about the risks of *not* participating in these activities? An article in the *Deseret News* states that "the life of an American teenager is risky business. Nearly a third of high school students drink regularly and a quarter had a physical fight within a year. They may live or die from consequences related to tobacco, alcohol, and drug use; unhealthy diets, physical inactivity, and whether they brawl or carry weapons." The same survey shows that attempted suicide continues to increase.[21]

My heart continues to bleed for the tens of thousands youth nationwide who are held in custody today, just as it did when I first saw that arch of shoes. After four decades, to hear the SideKicks express their appreciation for their high school rodeo opportunities has been an enlightening and rewarding experience.

Was it worth the risk? Absolutely. Nothing ventured, nothing gained.

Questions to Ponder

1. Someone once mentioned that this book was about a rodeo advisor putting his high school students on mean bulls and bucking horses as part of the school's extracurricular activity. After reading this book, what might your response to that perspective be?

2. Before rodeo was introduced at North Sanpete High, some students seemed to have lost interest in school. Some were on the verge of dropping out. With high school rodeo as an option, they became excited about being in school again. What value do you place on innovative programs designed to help students find their place in society, even those programs that break century-old traditions?

3. Four brothers playing high school football each received injuries: a herniated disk, a shoulder injury, an ankle injury, and a fractured vertebra and bulging disc. Their father said, "It makes you wonder why we support and endorse a sport that has a high potential to cripple our youth."[22] Realizing that this might apply equally to high school rodeo, how do you feel about this father's concern?

4. High school rodeo is not sanctioned by the State Athletic Association and is managed by parents. Should school districts become more supportive of high school rodeo?

5. Lynn Stoddard, a retired educator and author of *Educating for Human Greatness,* compares two educational philosophies. He says that rather than attempting to make students alike in knowledge and skills, our aim should be to nurture human diversity—that is, to help students discover and develop their unique talents and gifts.[23] No doubt, the latter builds self-confidence

and self-esteem more than when teachers focus on a student's weaknesses through remediation. Considering both areas to be important, where do you think schools should place more emphasis?

6. High school rodeo became a vehicle that enabled some difficult students to no longer be difficult. What are your feelings in regard to seeing innovations that will capture interest for even, and perhaps especially, the difficult student, made available in a high school program?

7. Perhaps there are other messages in this SideKick adventure story that are "waiting in the wings" for students, parents, schoolteachers, school administrators, and rodeo personnel. What do you think these messages may be?

8. How do you feel about this comment from Albert Einstein: "Only a life lived for others is a life worthwhile"?[24]

Appendix

"New Rodeo Club at North Sanpete High"

Designed to promote and preserve the tradition of early Western America with the sport of rodeo while building the character of youth, North Sanpete High School has established a rodeo club. The club was organized Monday after receiving approval from Principal Howard K. Lay, Superintendent Royal Allred and the North Sanpete School board.

This club will join with other high school clubs in the state and nation by becoming members of the National High School Rodeo Association. This association consists of 10,000 members from 26 other states and two Canadian Provinces. The local club will offer the students an opportunity to develop and practice rodeo skills. They will also be able to compete in rodeos throughout the State beginning this school year.

The rodeo program consists of voluntary memberships designed to develop leadership, sportsmanship, citizenship and human relations. Students who are to participate in the events must maintain grade standards set by the State Athletic Association and must be in good standing with the school. The club is also open to students who may choose not to participate in the events but want to enjoy and appreciate the sport of rodeo more fully.

According to Mr. Thomas, many of our top cowboys in professional rodeo today started in high school competition, then moved into college competition and on to professional rodeos. College scholarships are granted through the Foundation so young people involved in high school rodeo may be assisted in furthering their education.He pointed out to parents that any students who wishes to participate in the rodeos must have a notarized parent consent. He stated that a membership fee included student insurance.

    —*The Mount Pleasant Pyramid*, March 1976

SideKicks Roster, 1976–1981

Robert Draper, saddle bronc; Danny Livingston, bareback bronc; Dale Peel, bull riding; Casey Blackburn, bareback bronc; John Larsen, bull riding; Val Lynch, bull riding, bareback bronc, saddle bronc, team roping; Kelly Poulsen, bareback bronc; Darryl Peel, bull riding, bareback bronc; Kevin Thompson, bareback bronc; Shari Stevens, pole bending, goat tying, barrel racing; Ann Mickkelsen, barrel racing, pole bending, goat tying, queen contest; Kellie Simons, goat tying; Robyn Ruiz, barrel racing, pole bending; Crystal Watson, barrel racing, pole bending, goat tying; Leesa Rasmussen, pole bending, barrel racing; Casey Larsen, bareback bronc; Bert Miner, bareback bronc; Tim Larsen, bull riding; Richard Rigby, bull riding; Clint Lynch, bull riding, bareback bronc; Glen Terry (Shorty), bull riding, bareback bronc; Jimmy Christensen, bareback bronc; Tim Tidwell, bareback bronc; Dean Daniels, bull riding; Robert Hiller, bull riding; Wade "Huggy" Lynch, saddle bronc; Garth Edmunds, bareback bronc; Tony Tucker, bareback bronc; Jon Larsen, bull riding, bareback bronc, saddle bronc; Lauren Larsen, bull riding, bareback bronc, saddle bronc; Blake Nielsen, bull riding, bareback bronc, saddle bronc riding; Jerry Lynch, bareback bronc, saddle bronc; David Breaux, bull riding, bareback bronc; Wade Christensen, bull riding; Heidi McKay, barrel racing, pole bending, goat tying, queen contest; Dawn Bynum, barrel racing, pole bending, goat tying, queen contest; Carol Roseman, barrel racing, pole bending, goat tying, queen contest; Alana Bynum, barrel racing, pole bending, goat tying, queen contest; Sheri Christensen, barrel racing, pole bending, barrel racing; Anita Mollinet, barrel racing, pole bending, goat tying; Torie Poulsen, barrel racing, pole bending, goat tying; Lesa Brewer, barrel racing, pole bending, goat tying.

My apologies if I've left anyone off the list. Those not mentioned in *SideKicks* have their own stories that could have been shared. They too played a vital part in the making of SideKick history at North Sanpete High School. I realized there were so many who contributed as I browsed through the high school yearbooks during that era. They too made history as this club became one of the most popular innovations at North Sanpete High. Each of them remains an unsung hero.

"Cowboy Essence . . . Every Day!"

Cowboy Essence is the self-satisfaction in knowing you did your best to become the best you are capable of becoming. The cowboy culture has long been admired for many wonderful characteristics: hard work, integrity, ambition, self-reliance, family values, confidence, honesty, loyalty, having a relationship with the season of the year, and perseverance through hard times as well as gratitude during the good times. We are fortunate to have the cowboy culture to remind us of Cowboy Essence. But no matter who we are or where we are in our lives, we all have the opportunity to demonstrate these qualities. Examples are everywhere as the spirit of the American Cowboy filters into all aspects of our communities, culture, and society, whether we are a schoolteacher, physician, firefighter, law enforcement officer, businessperson, civil service worker, outdoor recreationist, student, or family member at home.

—"The Constitution of the Babbitt Ranches," Article
III; used with written permission from the historic
Babbitt Ranches of Arizona

"A Cowboys' Prayer"

Heavenly Father, we pause, mindful of the many blessings you have bestowed upon us. We ask that You be with us at this rodeo and we pray that You will guide us in this arena of life. We don't ask for special favors, we don't ask to draw around a chute-fightin' horse, to never break a barrier. Nor do we ask for all daylight runs or not to draw a steer that don't lay. Help us, Lord, to live our lives in such a manner that when we make that last inevitable ride up there, where the grass grows lush, green, and stirrup high, and the water runs cool, clean and deep, that you, my Lord, as our last judge, will tell us our entry fees are paid.

— Clem McSpadden

Note: SideKicks high school rodeo announcer Jay Quarnberg often read this prayer at the beginning of high school rodeos.

"SideKicks Hit the Dirt in Moab"

Members of the "SideKicks" North Sanpete High School's rodeo club opened the rodeo season last Saturday at the San Juan High School arena in Moab. Glen Terry, club president, who had taken first place honors in the bull riding event at the Utah Barrel Racing Jackpot in Spanish Fork in March, was the only SideKick to place in an event. Terry drew the same bull, "Rawhide," that he had at Spanish Fork. He lost position to the left during the ride, but made a remarkable comeback, making a qualified ride that gave him fifth-place honors. SideKick Vice-president, Rusty Bench, drew a bull called "Scotch Highlander." The bull caught his horn on the way out of the chute and Rusty got a re-ride. The second time out, Rusty held on almost to the buzzer, which sounded as he hit the dirt. The other SideKicks had trouble hanging on as they gained experience. Danny Livingston, Val Lynch, and Casey Blackburn competed in the bareback bronc competition but were unable to outlast the clock.

—*The Mount Pleasant Pyramid,* April 1976

"Local Cowboys Win Top Honors in High School Rodeo Finals"

Blake Nielsen and Lauren Larsen won top honors in bareback bronc riding at the Utah State High School Rodeo Finals in Heber City. They will compete at the National Finals Rodeo in Huron, North Dakota, July 27–August 6, for the National High School Bareback Bronc Riding Championship.

Nielsen won a first-place award in the second go-round. He made an outstanding ride in the final go-round at Heber City to claim first place. He is now ranked as the top bareback bronc rider in the Utah State High School Rodeo Association for 1978.

Larsen won the first go-round, took second in the second go-round. She ended up as the second-place high school bareback bronc rider in the State.

—*The Mount Pleasant Pyramid,* August 1976

"History of the SideKicks"

The North Sanpete High School Rodeo Club (the SideKicks) was organized in March of 1976. Club officers elected were Glen Terry, President; Rusty Bench; Vice President; Karen Anderson, Secretary and Casey Blackburn, treasurer.

The following year they, with Rusty Bench, President; John Larsen, Vice President; Sharie Stevens, Secretary; Ann Mikkelsen, Treasurer; and Kellie Simons, Historian, sponsored their first high school rodeo. Qualifying for the State High School Rodeo Finals were: Rusty Bench and Robert Draper, Saddle Bronc Riding; Tim Larsen, Bull Riding; Val Lynch, Bareback Bronc Riding and Ann Mikkelsen, Queen Contest. Robert won at State. He became the club's first to qualify for the National High School Finals Rodeo. Last year, Rusty won the All-around Cowboy Award at the North Sanpete High School Second Annual Rodeo. Qualifying that year for State were Rusty Bench, Bull Riding and Saddle Bronc; Jimmy Christensen, Lauren Larsen and Blake Nielsen, Bareback Bronc Riding and Crystal Watson, Barrel Racing and Pole Bending and Heidi McKay in the Queen Contest. She was chosen second attendant at State.

Blake won first-place honors at State and Lauren placed second in the Bareback Bronc Riding. Blake went on to win third-place honors in the second go-round in the Bareback Riding competition at the National Level in Huron, S.D. Lauren also competed at that National Finals High School Rodeo.

One of last year's highlights was having Mickey Young visit North Sanpete. He was the current runner-up to the World's Bareback Bronc Riding Championship in Pro Rodeo that year. Mickey presented a bronc riding seminar at the arena during each of three days. On the final day, in the evening, he was the guest speaker at a banquet at the High School.

This year's special guest at North Sanpete was Don Gay, four-time World Champion Bull Rider. Gay gave an excellent Bull Riding Seminar. Friday evening, he was the guest speaker at the Club's Annual Banquet. The club has received immense amount of greatly appreciated support from the School District, High School Rodeo Officials, sponsors and fans. They express their thanks and appreciation to all who have helped their dreams to become a reality.

—In the SideKicks third annual high school rodeo
souvenir program, May 26, 28, 1979

"The Best in Sanpete"

The North Sanpete High School rodeo club had its beginning four years ago when Mr. Reed Thomas, a native of Wales, Utah, moved back to Sanpete County and joined the faculty at North Sanpete High School. The club had sponsored several successful rodeos and has seen several of its members qualify for State Finals and some went on to the National Finals. In 1978, Lauren Larsen and Blake Nielsen of Ephraim both qualified for and rode in the National Finals Rodeo Finals in Huron, South Dakota.

This year, six members of the NSHS Rodeo Club qualified for the State Finals Rodeo in Heber City, Utah, June 19–23. Jimmy Christensen, Mt. Pleasant, was qualified in bareback bronc riding; Jon Larsen and Blake Nielsen, Ephraim, Ephraim, were both qualified in three events—saddle bronc, bareback, and bulls. Heidi McKay, Carol Roseman, and JoAnn Bigler were all qualified in the Queen Contest. Heidi was chosen runner-up to the queen and JoAnn was voted Miss Congeniality.

The North Sanpete High Rodeo Club has been open to all high school students in Sanpete County since the other high schools have not participated in this program. NSHS Rodeo Club members greatly appreciate the support given to their rodeos and projects by the people of Sanpete County.

—In the Sanpete County fair book, August 1979

"Another SideKick Banner Year"

The SideKick girls sponsored a goat tying seminar in the spring of '79. Taught by Shannon Lewis, a National High School Rodeo Finals qualifier, they held that seminar in Heidi McKay's barn. Several girls, who were members of the SideKick club, attended this one day's event.

More and more SideKicks cowgirls began contesting in high school rodeo events this year. In order for them to get involved, it did require full parental support. This required a trained horse, transportation, and outfits to wear for those entering the queen contests.

This year, thirty-three students had joined the SideKicks Club with twenty-two being paid members of the State and National High School Rodeo Association. Those card-carrying members were active contestants in rodeos throughout the State that year.Heidi McKay was chosen by a panel of judges to reign as 1st. Attendant over the Tooele High School Rodeo. That same week-end, she was chosen 2nd. Attendant to reign over the Grand County High School Rodeo in Moab. Heidi also placed fifth in the goat tying event in Tooele.

Blake Nielsen won 1st place honors in bull riding in Moab. He also took first place honors in bareback bronc riding at the Riverton High School Rodeo.

At the North Sevier High School Rodeo in Richfield, JoAnn Bigler, a freshman at North Sanpete High, was chosen to reign

as 2nd Attendant. She, also, was chosen to receive the Congeniality Award, making her the first member of the SideKicks to
receive this award.

At North Sevier, Jimmy Christensen brought home fourth
place honors in bareback bronc riding. Winning first place
honors in bareback bronc riding at the Uintah High School
Rodeo in Vernal was Blake Nielsen. He won a first place in saddle
bronc riding at the Dixie High School Rodeo in St. George. Jon
Larsen took second place honors at the same rodeo. Blake also
won second in the bull riding while Jon brought home third place
in the saddle bronc riding contest. Heidi McKay was chosen to
reign as 1st. Attendant at the Dixie High School Rodeo

"Slash C Rodeo Company, Inc."

"Slash C Rodeo Company of Francis, Utah had its beginning
in Mt. Pleasant in their old arena," Bill Crittenden said. "The first
rodeo we ever put on was at Mt. Pleasant. It was at their 4th of
July Rodeo in 1975. For $1500 we provided the livestock, the
clowns, the pickup men and the judges. I was twenty years old
when some members of the local riding club signed that contract
with us. I was thrilled as we took on our first rodeo contract."

Known as the "Hub City Days Rodeo," that became the first
semi pro-rodeo to be held in Mt. Pleasant. It has since continued
on an annual basis with Slash C Rodeo Company being their
stock contractor for several years.

Bill continued, "My father had taken a load of horses back
to Tennessee. He sold them to the Longhorn Rodeo Company
owned by Country Music Superstar Loretta Lynn. That money
is what got us into the rodeo business. We went to Texas and
purchased some of Neal Gay's bulls."

Bill also mentioned he had gone to Miles City, Montana, for bucking horses. On another occasion, he flew in a single-engine plane to Blanco, New Mexico, and landed in a field on a ranch. From that trip, "Rodeo Red," "Powder Keg," "#76," and "#155," some of his top bucking bulls, were purchased. The fact remains, Slash C had accumulated some mighty good bucking stock. This rodeo stock became a working part of the SideKick sponsored high school rodeos, seminars and practice events. Slash C Rodeos played an important role with the success of the SideKicks and the first dozen years plus of Mt. Pleasant's City's "Hub City Days" Rodeo, Annual 4th of July celebrations. That celebration continues to flourish today, thanks to the efforts of many down through the years. With additional seating added a few years ago, they now seat as many as 2500 spectators at this annual semiprofessional rodeo.

"Bar T Rodeo Company"

The Bar T Rodeo Company was founded in the Red Rocks of Moab sixty years ago by Cowboy Hall of Famer D.A. Swanny Kirby and his wife Verda. Swanny brought some of the earlier top rodeos to Utah. He produced quality PRCA rodeos in other parts of the the United States, also. He took bucking stock to the first National Finals Rodeo in Dallas, Texas in 1959. Bar T has continued to furnish bucking stock at every National Finals Rodeo since.

Their son Bud and his wife, Evelyn, built a breeding program that today has one of the most sought after horse herds in the world. Today, the Bar T Rodeo Company has been passed to the third generation and is owned by Jeff and Wendy Flitten along with their son, Cody, a fourth generation family member.

Today, Bar T continues to win its share of top bucking stock awards in Pro Rodeo.

Twelve years ago, Jeff and Wendy started a bull breeding program. Since then, several of the bulls they have raised have been selected to go to the Wrangler National Finals Rodeo in Las Vegas, Nevada. They now call Sanpete County, home of the SideKicks, their home.

In Memory of Little Joe

The youngest in a long line of cowboy boots,
You hit the ground running
To place your picture on the wall
In the siblings Rodeo Hall of Fame.
From Little Buckaroos to
State Finals
All four years of high school
Your fame grew in the family circle.
At nineteen, to the Lord you turned,
Giving two years of service
To gather God's flock.
Upon returning to suppressed hopes and dreams,
Rising to the top,
Plagued with physical pain.
"Cowboy up" is all you thought,
"A little pain, not to mind,
Get up! There's work!"
As a last resort, you turned to modern medicine
Only to find a lump on your spine.
A biopsy run and the worst confirmed.

On your second round of chemo,
Your future dim,
Cancer eclipsed your earthly soul.
Death gives birth to flee this earthly home,
Cinch the riggin' tight
When the gate swings wide.
Watch out for the comet's fiery tail
As you spur across the star-lit sky.

—Jerald King

Note: Joe Allred, a former student of North Sanpete High School, rode saddle broncs under the banner of the Sanpete County High School Rodeo Club, forerunner of the SideKicks. He passed away of cancer in 2006. This poem was written and read at his funeral by Jerald King.

A SideKick's Hat

I hope to wear a cowboy hat in heaven.
Not sure there's a halo in my size.
On street of gold, I'd be lost.
Just give me my hat,
A good bronc, bull or horse,
And an arena full of dirt.
The smell of hair after a summer rain.
I'd be in heaven for sure.
No need for all that fancy stuff.
A sky full of stars,
A full moon
I could sing to
For those rainy days,

I put some stars in my
Pockets to pass the time away.
Oh Lord, I don't need much
I'm just an old Side Kick riding up
To those pearly gates.

—Jerald King

"A Glimpse into Cowboy Heaven" (1986)

An array of glittering lights suddenly came into view as we approached the crest of the hill overlooking Las Vegas, the "entertainment capital of the world" and the new home of the National Finals Rodeo. My heart kicked out a couple of extra beats as my foot pressed a little further on the accelerator.

Arriving at the Thomas and Mack Center just in time for a spectator display of lights, music, and sound, the NFR for '86 had just began. After the announcer had given a rip roaring intro-duction, country music singer Reba McIntyre sang so beautiful our National Anthem, renewing my love and appreciation for the great nation in which we live. The rodeo continued, excitement grew and spectators moved a little closer to the edge of their seats as we watched the best in rodeo compete for world titles.

Lewis Fields, the All-round Champ from Elkridge, Utah, made it appear easy as he took the lead in bareback bronc riding. Later, he proved that even champions get thrown as he made an early exit from his saddle bronc.

Monty "Hawkeye" Hensen, known for landing on his feet after making many great saddle bronc rides, landed on his head inside chute #6. As that bronc started to react to Hawkeye's sudden appearance, the crowd became silent. The gateman made an attempt to unlatch the chute gate, to free that horse, but failed. After what seemed like forever, the gate finally opened on a second attempt. The horse dashed out into the arena. The cowgirl sitting next to me shed a tear. The crowd remained silent as a sickening chill was felt . . . the feeling of a tragedy. After a long moment, Hawkeye walked out of that chute with his hands in the air, his way of telling us, "I'm okay." The crowd went wild as excitement found only in rodeo continued.

The Cowboy Christmas Trade Show really got things stirred up inside of me. It was a back in time experience, back to my boyhood days when I would browse through the Christmas catalog wishing for most everything. There were beautiful custom saddles, western paintings and sculptures, western apparel and all kinds of cowboy paraphernalia. I found myself struggling to keep my credit card in my pocket so that my children might be able to enjoy Christmas. Country-western sound was abundant throughout, top names such as George Strait, Mickey Gilley, Meryl Haggart, Willey Nelsen, and Reba McIntyre, to name a few. After a great eating experience at the Landmark, Moe Bandy got us all "hyped up" on country sounds.

Sunday morning, cowboys and cowgirls from everywhere gathered together at the rodeo arena for "Cowboy Church." It was there where my wife commented, "You Cowboys are sure unique. You have your own kind of entertainment, your own style of dress, your own type of music, and your own way of showing your love for country, your fellowman, and God." It then hit me . . . that weekend I had captured a glimpse of "Cowboy Heaven."

—Reed Thomas, *Horse Talk News,* Las Vegas,
Nevada, December 20, 1986

In Memory of a SideKick

A Black Cowboy Hat

*In granite stands a reminder to all how fragile every breath
    can be.*
Bumps and bruises, some unseen.
Others, the whole world to see.
Under a black cowboy hat, a little giant stood
*Who, in the growing pains, could have chosen different
    paths to ride.*
Chose SideKicks and took the one less traveled.
Learned that fear is only large to overshadow dreams
If one is not afraid to grab life by the horns.
On a dusty road, Clint found a friend
To pull him out of the sand.
The very chain that rescued him
Now sent him to ride rough stock for the Lord.
May the riggin' stay tight
To keep the devil's herd from increasing numbers
Until we meet again.
I tip my hat to a fallen friend.
May God be with you, a giant little man.

—Jerald King
In memory of Clint Erin Lynch, 1962–1996

Acknowledgments

An author does not like to admit to a poor memory. However, at first it appeared that was what I had been hobbled with as the SideKick story began to unfold. It was amazing how many of the memories did come back to life as the SideKicks shared their stories—first as only a blur but then developing into vivid pictures. However, some of the finer details of the SideKicks' competitions remain a product of my imagination.

I am especially grateful to my wife, Robyn. She edited my writing, jotting down notes with words such as *cut, boring, good,* and *very good.* Her attention to detail kept me from getting carried away with my muse.

I am so grateful to those SideKicks who were willing to relive this journey with me, sharing their memories and expressing their feelings. After many years gone by, it was a wonderful experience to reconnect. Memories were taken from the club scrapbooks, from *The Mount Pleasant Pyramid,* and from the annual high school yearbooks of that era. Most helpful were the one-on-one interviews they so graciously granted.

In the beginning of this SideKick adventure, Jim Thornton was vice principal of North Sanpete High School. He later served as principal and then became a district superintendent. My heartfelt thanks to him for the support he rendered to the SideKicks and for writing the foreword of this book.

I also remain indebted to photographer Bryan Strain, whose talents are displayed on the cover of this book and elsewhere. His input adds a new dimension to this story that brings the text of *SideKicks* to a higher level.

I also appreciate Jerald King, a friend and neighbor in our farming operations, for contributing his poetic talent and also taking this story to the next level.

I don't consider myself a hero. I simply did the job I was given. *SideKicks* is not about me. It's about the SideKicks who continue to be heroes. They are the ones who faced their fears with courage. They are the ones who took advantage of the opportunities that came their way. They are the ones who took charge of their lives in a positive sense and have remained good citizens through the years.

This story would never have taken place without the support of the local school board members, several school administrators, the community, and my generous sponsors.

And many thanks to Eschler Editing—Angela Eschler, Kathy Gordon, Michele Preisendorf, and Heidi Brockbank—for their talented assistance. Also, Jason Robinson at Atlas Graphics and Ben Welch for their design expertise, as well as the many friends and family who helped in innumerable ways.

This story is a reality because of a team effort. You are all greatly appreciated.

Notes

[1] Goodreads, accessed March 21, 2016, http://www.goodreads.com/quotes/24499-be-the-change-that-you-wish-to-see-in-the.

[2] Eric Schulzke, "Gates Says Education Reform Is Tougher Than Battling Polio, Malaria, tuberculosis," *Deseret News,* July 3, 2014, A5.

[3] Goodreads, accessed March 8, 2016, http://www.goodreads.com/quotes/2528-keep-away-from-people-who-try-to-belittle-your-ambitions.

[4] "Booker T. Washington Quotes," Wisdom of the Wise.com, accessed March 8, 2016, http://www.wisdom-of-the-wise.com/Booker-T-Washington.htm.

[5] New York: Aladdin Paperbacks, 1954.

[6] Katheryn B. Brown, "Cowboys Are the Toughest Athletes Around," *Pendleton Round-Up, East Oregonian,* Sept. 2014, 4.

[7] New York, Simon and Schuster, 1960.

[8] In "North San Pete High School: Big Rodeo from a Little School," World of Rodeo and Western Heritage, vol. 2, no. 9, May 10, 1978, 12.

[9] Lane Creer-Harris, "Wright Rodeo Dynasty Continues," Fiesta Days souvenir program, J-Mark Printing, 2014.

[10] Greg Knight, "Humphries Wins National Rodeo Championship," *Sanpete Messenger,* Aug. 14, 2014, A9.

[11] Stephen R. Covey Home, accessed March 17, 2016, https://www.stephencovey.com/7habits/7habits-habit2.php.

[12] Paul S. Edwards, "Dropout Consequences," *Deseret News,* A8, Oct. 22, 2014, A8; August 13, 2014, C6.

[13] *Death in the Afternoon,* New York: Scribner, 1932, 153.

[14] Paul S. Edwards, "School Innovations Require Not Just Funding, but Latitude to Move from Current 'Factory Model,'" *Deseret News,* Feb. 4, 2015, A8.

[15] Kate Kellan, "Study Finds Poverty Reduces Brain Power," Reuters, Aug. 29, 2013, http://www.reuters.com/article/us-poverty-brain-idUSBRE97S10W20130829.

[16] Lane Anderson, "Research Finds Being Poor Can Hurt Brain," *Deseret News,* July 7, 2014, A1.

[17] Amy McDonald, "Technology Not a Silver Bullet for Poverty, Inequality," *Deseret News,* Aug. 9, 2014, A3.

[18] Eric Schulzke, "Educating Max," *Deseret News,* Feb. 8, 2015, A1.

[19] Steve Densley, "Live Your Life Looking Forward," *Daily Herald,* Sept. 21, 2014, C5.

[20] Patrick Mulvihill, "No Pain, No Fame," *Pendleton Round-Up,* Sept, 10–13, 2014, 6, published by the East Oregonian.

[21] Lois M. Collins, "Risky Business: The Life of an American Teenager," *Deseret News,* Aug. 9, 2014, A5.

[22] Blain Layton, "High School Football Costs," Readers' Forum letters, *Deseret News.*

[23] Lynn Stoddard, *Educating for Human Greatness* (Florida: Peppertree Press, 2010), xxiii.

[24] Goodreads, accessed March 21, 2016, http://www.goodreads.com/quotes/16909-only-a-life-lived-for-others-is-a-life-worthwhile.

Reed Thomas (Photo Credit: Bryan Strain)

About the Author

Reed Thomas self-published "Golden Re-Connections," a memoir he freely distributed to family and friends. Though he's spent most of his life as an educator, he's also enjoyed living the life of the American cowboy. Now he reconnects with some of his past in SideKicks. He shares with the public how this lifestyle turned good high school boys into great men. Here is a refreshing contrast to the tens of thousands of our nation's boys being held in custody today.

He and his wife of nearly fifty years have built themselves a nest in the mountains of central Utah as well as in the hills of Oklahoma. They are the proud parents of five children, fourteen grandchildren, and two great-grandchildren.

* * *

A portion of the royalties from this book will be dedicated to helping kids succeed against the odds. This campaign is to be accomplished through a network of private citizens, public officials, business leaders, and others interested in lending their support. Join us with your stories, support, and suggestions at Kids Succeeding against the Odds (www.succeedingagainstodds.org).

Made in the USA
Columbia, SC
20 June 2023

18415281R00138